HomeBuilders Couples Series ®

growing

☑ **W9-BUE-675**

Together

in Christ

By David Sunde

FAMILYLIFE™
Bringing Timeless Principles Home
Little Rock, Arkansas

Group
Loveland, Colorado

Group's R.E.A.L. Guarantee® to you:

This Group resource incorporates our R.E.A.L. approach to ministry—one that encourages long-term retention and life transformation. It's ministry that's:

Relational
Because learner-to-learner interaction enhances learning and builds Christian friendships.

Experiential
Because what learners experience through discussion and action sticks with them up to 9 times longer than what they simply hear or read.

Applicable
Because the aim of Christian education is to equip learners to be both hearers and doers of God's Word.

Learner-based
Because learners understand and retain more when the learning process takes into consideration how they learn best.

Visit our Web site: **www.grouppublishing.com**

Credits
FamilyLife
Editor: David Boehi
Assistant Editor: Julie Denker

Group Publishing, Inc.
Editor: Matt Lockhart
Creative Development Editor: Paul Woods
Chief Creative Officer: Joani Schultz
Copy Editor: Janis Sampson
Art Director: Jenette L. McEntire
Cover Art Director: Jeff A. Storm
Computer Graphic Artist: Anita M. Cook
Cover Photographer: Tony Stone Images
Illustrator: Ken Jacobsen
Production Manager: Peggy Naylor

ISBN 0-7644-2243-X
20 19 18 17   09 08 07 06 05

Printed in the United States of America.

How to Let the Lord Build Your House
and not labor in vain

●

The HomeBuilders Couples Series®: A small-group Bible study dedicated to making your family all that God intended.

FamilyLife is a division of Campus Crusade for Christ International, an evangelical Christian organization founded in 1951 by Bill Bright. FamilyLife was started in 1976 to help fulfill the Great Commission by strengthening marriages and families and then equipping them to go to the world with the gospel of Jesus Christ. The FamilyLife Marriage Conference is held in most major cities throughout the United States and is one of the fastest-growing marriage conferences in America today. "FamilyLife Today," a daily radio program hosted by Dennis Rainey, is heard on hundreds of stations across the country. Information on all resources offered by FamilyLife may be obtained by contacting us at the address, telephone number, or World Wide Web site listed below.

Dennis Rainey, Executive Director
FamilyLife
P.O. Box 8220
Little Rock, AR 72221-8220
1-800-FL-TODAY
www.familylife.com

A division of Campus Crusade for Christ International
Bill Bright, Founder and President

112078

About the Sessions

Each session in this study is composed of the following categories: Warm-Up, Blueprints, Wrap-Up, and HomeBuilders Project. A description of each of these categories follows:

Warm-Up (15 minutes)

 The purpose of Warm-Up is to help people unwind from a busy day and get to know each other better. Typically the first point in Warm-Up is an exercise that is meant to be fun while introducing the topic of the session. The ability to share in fun with others is important in building relationships. Another component of Warm-Up is the Project Report (except in Session One), which is designed to provide accountability for the HomeBuilders Project that is to be completed by couples between sessions.

Blueprints (60 minutes)

 This is the heart of the study. In this part of each session, people answer questions related to the topic of study and look to God's Word for understanding. Some of the questions are to be answered by couples, in subgroups, or in the group at large. There are notes in the margin or instructions within a question that designate these groupings.

Wrap-Up (15 minutes)

This category serves to "bring home the point" and wind down a session in an appropriate fashion.

HomeBuilders Project (60 minutes)

This project is the unique application step in a HomeBuilders study. Before leaving a meeting, couples are encouraged to "Make a Date" to do this project prior to the next meeting. Each HomeBuilders Project contains three sections: 1) As a Couple—a brief exercise designed to get the date started in a fun way; 2) Individually—a section of questions for husbands and wives to answer separately; 3) Interact as a Couple—an opportunity for couples to share their answers with each other and to make application in their lives.

In addition to the above regular features, occasional activities are labeled "For Extra Impact." These are activities that generally provide a more active or visual way to make a particular point. Be mindful that people within a group have different learning styles. While most of what is presented is verbal, a visual or active exercise now and then helps engage more of the senses and appeals to people who learn best by seeing, touching, and doing.

About the Author

Dave Sunde has served with Campus Crusade for Christ since 1966. He is a writer for Promise Keepers and writer-developer for Marketplace CrossTalk. He and Sande, his wife, are graduates of Western Michigan University. Dave also has a graduate degree from Dallas Theological Seminary. The Sundes presently are helping to bring FamilyLife to the developing nations of the world. They live in Louisville, Colorado, in the Denver area and have three married daughters.

Contents

Acknowledgments **8**

Foreword **10**

Introduction **11**

A Word About Growing Together **14**

Session One: Essentials for Establishing
    Growth as a Couple..**15**

Session Two: The Power of Prayer in Marriage..................**27**

Session Three: The Guidebook for Growth **37**

Session Four: Growing Together Through the Holy Spirit....**49**

Session Five: Following Jesus..**61**

Session Six: Making Disciples **71**

Where Do You Go From Here? **83**

Our Problems, God's Answers...**87**

Leader's Notes **99**

Prayer Journal **124**

Recommended Reading...**128**

Acknowledgments

A vision for this HomeBuilders study was born in my heart many years ago when FamilyLife was just getting underway. As Dennis Rainey and I talked, we recognized that a firm grasp of how to live the Christian life is absolutely key to the success of any marriage. We can predict great success for a marriage when there is sound, practical knowledge of both the Creator's design and his power to lead the marriage into the highest halls of human happiness. So in 1988 when plans started coming together under Dennis Rainey's leadership, I felt a deep gratitude to him and the FamilyLife team.

Thank you, Dennis, for your perseverance to see the vision become reality. You and Barbara are models of what it means to grow together in Christ during the years of your marriage.

It is a great honor and joy to work with the FamilyLife team. From the rough sketches of our ideas and outlines to the final copy, Dave Boehi and Julie Denker have been truly indispensable.

Dave's creative gifts ensured that we were expressing our thoughts in the most effective manner. His major editing work defined for me the pursuit of excellence.

Julie's warm encouragement, faithful coordination of the production, and tenacity with the deadlines kept us moving in the right direction. Thank you, Dave and Julie. I could not have done this without you.

I want to extend a very special word of thanks to the couples who met together in communities across America to field-test this study in its formative days. Your feedback and insights gave us invaluable counsel in revising the material.

To my lifetime companion, Sande, my wife, a heart full of thanks for the partnership in testing the teaching of this book in our years together. By God's power and love, we are growing together in Christ.

Foreword

One of the most dangerous assumptions a Christian could ever make is that spiritual growth will just happen. Far too many Christians today become stale and stagnant because they assume that growth will occur just because they are involved in religious activities. But the New Testament teaches that spiritual growth is the result of some basic and fundamental steps that each of us as Christians are responsible to take.

Dave Sunde has been a personal friend of mine for many years, and he is no newcomer to this subject of spiritual growth. He not only brings over thirty years of experience in biblical teaching to this subject, but he also shows a rock-solid walk with Christ in his own life. In the following six sessions, you will find that he captures the simple but profound essence of spiritual growth.

As in other studies in the HomeBuilders Couples Series, Dave eloquently demonstrates that spiritual growth best occurs as we are accountable to one another—to our spouses. I am thrilled that he has put these truths together in such a way that married couples who work through this study will be challenged to grow deeper in Christ.

Dennis Rainey

Executive Director, FamilyLife

Introduction

When a man and woman are married, they stand before a room of witnesses and proclaim their commitment to a lifetime of love. They recite a sacred vow "to have and to hold...from this day forward...to love, honor, and cherish...for better, for worse...for richer, for poorer...in sickness and in health...as long as we both shall live."

It's a happy day, perhaps the happiest in their lives. And yet, once the honeymoon ends, once the emotions of courtship and engagement subside, many couples realize that "falling in love" and building a good marriage are two different things. Keeping those vows is much more difficult than they thought it would be.

Otherwise intelligent people, who would not think of buying a car, investing money, or even going to the grocery store without some initial planning, enter into marriage with no plan of how to make that relationship succeed.

But God has already provided the plan, a set of blueprints for building a truly God-honoring marriage. His plan is designed to enable a man and woman to grow together in a mutually satisfying relationship and then to reach out to others with the love of Christ. Ignoring this plan leads only to isolation and separation between husband and wife. It's a pattern evident in so many homes today: Failure to follow God's blueprints results in wasted effort, bitter disappointment, and, in far too many cases, divorce.

In response to this need in marriages today, FamilyLife has developed a series of small-group studies called the HomeBuilders Couples Series.

You could complete this study alone with your spouse, but we strongly urge you to either form or join a group of couples studying this material. You will find that the questions in each session not only help you grow closer to your spouse, but they help create a special environment of warmth and fellowship as you study together how to build the type of marriage you desire. Participating in a HomeBuilders group could be one of the highlights of your married life.

The Bible: Your Blueprints for a God-Honoring Marriage

You will notice as you proceed through this study that the Bible is used frequently as the final authority on issues of life and marriage. Although written thousands of years ago, this Book still speaks clearly and powerfully about the conflicts and struggles faced by men and women. The Bible is God's Word— his blueprints for building a God-honoring home and for dealing with the practical issues of living.

We encourage you to have a Bible with you for each session. For this series we use the New International Version as our primary reference. Another excellent translation is the New American Standard Bible.

Ground Rules

Each group session is designed to be enjoyable and informative—and nonthreatening. Three simple ground rules will help ensure that everyone feels comfortable and gets the most out of the experience:

1. Don't share anything that would embarrass your spouse.

2. You may pass on any question you don't want to answer.

3. If possible, plan to complete the HomeBuilders Project as a couple between group sessions.

A Few Quick Notes About Leading a HomeBuilders Group

1. Leading a group is much easier than you may think! A group leader in a HomeBuilders session is really a "facilitator." As a leader, your goal is simply to guide the group through the discussion questions. You don't need to teach the material—in fact, we don't want you to! The special dynamic of a HomeBuilders group is that couples teach themselves.

2. This material is designed to be used in a home study, but it also can be adapted for use in a Sunday school environment. (See page 101 for more information about this option.)

3. We have included a section of Leader's Notes in the back of this book. Be sure to read through these notes before leading a session; they will help you prepare.

4. For more material on leading a HomeBuilders group, be sure to get a copy of the *HomeBuilders Leader Guide*, by Drew and Kit Coons. This book is an excellent resource that provides helpful guidelines on how to start a study, how to keep discussion moving, and much more.

A Word About Growing Together

To summarize the Christian life in six interactive sessions is somewhat like trying to summarize the Olympic Games. A listing of events, the competitors, and the locations of the events is essential, but there's more to the Olympics than a dry list. The drama of athletes experiencing "the thrill of victory and the agony of defeat," the deafening roar from the stadium, and the sense that history is being written make our hearts beat faster. To attend the Olympics is the privilege of a lifetime, and so is the experience of growing together in Christ.

In this study, you'll start the process of growing together in Christ. The essentials are here. But the actual living out of the principles is where you'll experience the real adventure.

Reality ensures that you will sometimes know the agony of defeat. But don't lose heart—the thrill of victory will come as you learn to let go of your selfish concerns and follow Christ together.

Athletes who qualify to compete in the Olympic Games have succeeded in mastering certain disciplines. In a similar way, as you grow together in spiritual oneness, you will be introduced to the necessary disciplines for spiritual growth.

But that is not the whole story. At the heart of growing together in the Lord is the incredible joy of actually coming to know God in a personal way. God has opened the way for us through Jesus Christ! I invite you to enjoy Christ even as countless couples have, who are now in the heavenly stadium cheering us on to victory.

David Sunde

Essentials for Establishing Growth as a Couple

The Christian life is one of exciting growth as you establish a solid relationship with Christ.

W A R M • U P   15   M I N U T E S

Meaningful Moments

Introduce yourselves as a couple by telling the group one of the following things about your relationship. Between the two of you, decide to share

- a particularly fun getaway or vacation you've had as a couple and what made it special or
- the most meaningful spiritual experience you've had as a couple.

Getting Connected

Pass your books around the room, and have each couple

write in their names, phone numbers, and e-mail addresses in the space provided.

_____
NAME, PHONE, & E-MAIL

_____
NAME, PHONE, & E-MAIL

_____
NAME, PHONE, & E-MAIL

_____
NAME, PHONE, & E-MAIL

_____
NAME, PHONE, & E-MAIL

_____
NAME, PHONE, & E-MAIL

_____
NAME, PHONE, & E-MAIL

BLUEPRINTS   60 MINUTES

Whether it is the rapid development of a newborn child or the first blossoming of a fruit tree, we naturally expect to see growth in all living things. Our life in Christ, too, is meant to be an exciting experience of growth.

Slow Growing

Case Study

Chuck's credentials were impeccable: He had received top grades in high school, had graduated with honors from Harvard, and had breezed through Harvard Medical School. He had successfully endured the grueling life of an intern and had completed a residency in pediatric surgery. When he began his private practice, it blossomed. He was confident, skilled, and well-liked.

When Chuck and his wife, Marcie, joined a local church, their pastor quickly tapped them for teaching and leadership roles. That's when the troubles began.

Marcie enthusiastically began teaching a Sunday school class for third graders, and it did very well. But soon after Chuck began teaching a class for young couples, class attendance began to fall.

"His teaching is weak," one couple said. "He hardly knows the Bible at all."

When the pastor asked Chuck how often he studied the Bible, Chuck replied, "Marcie seems to enjoy that more than I do. Besides, she has the freedom to attend weekly Bible studies. With my schedule, I would never have the time."

Chuck was also chairing a committee that was looking at options for building a new sanctuary. Soon the pastor began hearing reports of contention in the meetings.

"Chuck wants to run things his own way," one man said. "He blows up when anyone questions him."

While Chuck's pediatric clinic flourished, he seemed out of his element at church. "You'd never know that he's been a Christian for twenty years," his pastor said with a sigh.

If you have a large group, form smaller groups of about six people to answer the Blueprints questions. Unless otherwise noted, answer the questions in your subgroup. After finishing each section, take time for subgroups to share their answers with the whole group.

1. Why do you think Chuck seems immature for a twenty-year Christian?

Spiritual Growth

2. Read 1 Corinthians 3:1-3. What does it mean to be a spiritual "infant"?

3. What does a physical infant need to do to grow into a healthy, mature, well-balanced adult?

4. How would you compare this analogy to Christian growth? What do you think Christians need to do to become mature in their faith?

5. Read John 15:1-8. According to this passage, what is the key to spiritual growth? What does it mean to "remain" in Christ?

6. Read 2 Corinthians 5:17. In what ways do people become "new creations" when they become Christians? How do their lives change?

> **HomeBuilders Principle:**
> *The true Christian life is an exciting, daily relationship with the living Christ.*

Obstacles to Growth

7. What do you think prevents some Christians from growing spiritually? Look at Mark 4:1-9, 13-20 for additional thoughts. As people suggest answers to this question, make a list of those answers in the left-hand column.

Discuss the following four questions with the whole group.

8. Have you ever gone through a period in your life in which you didn't grow in your faith? If you can, tell about what characterized your life at that time. Why do you think you didn't grow?

Growing Together

9. You play a key role in your spouse's spiritual growth. What are some ways you can encourage your spouse in this area?

10. If both you and your spouse continue to grow *together* in your relationships with Christ, how will your growth affect your marriage?

11. What spiritual growth have you seen in your spouse's life since he or she became a Christian?

Answer questions 11 and 12 with your spouse. After answering, you may want to share an appropriate insight or discovery with the group.

12. In what areas do you hope to grow most in the next year?

HomeBuilders Principle:
As you each grow closer to God, you will experience greater oneness in your marriage.

W R A P • U P   15   M I N U T E S

Return to the list you made under question 7. Go over that list, and discuss how to work toward overcoming each of those obstacles in your lives. In the right-hand column under question 7, write down at least one solution for each obstacle.

Close your session with prayer, and make sure couples Make a Date for this session's HomeBuilders Project before they leave.

Make a Date

Make a date with your spouse to meet before the next session to complete the HomeBuilders Project. At the next session, your leader will ask you to share one thing from this experience.

DATE

TIME

LOCATION

HOMEBUILDERS PROJECT   6 0   M I N U T E S

As a Couple [10 minutes]
To begin your sharing, talk about couples on TV who provide bad examples of encouraging each other. Then talk about the real-life couples you know who are the best examples. Discuss what causes the differences between the two.

Individually [20 minutes]
1. Draw a graph that traces your spiritual growth

pattern since you became a Christian. Have your line go up during times of spiritual growth, flat during times of spiritual stagnation, and down during times of falling away from God.

High

M
A
T
U
R
I
T
Y

Low

TIME

When you
became a
Christian

Present

2. What factors have caused the various phases in your spiritual growth?

3. What are three things your spouse can do to help you grow spiritually?

Interact as a Couple [30 minutes]

1. Take a look at the spiritual growth charts you filled out, and explain your reasoning to each other.

2. Sometimes differing rates of Christian growth cause conflict between spouses. To what extent have you experienced this in your marriage? What can you do to work toward growing at similar rates in the future?

3. Share the answers each of you wrote for the other questions in the individual section.

4. Conclude your time together by writing a personal pledge statement, detailing what you commit to do during this course to make your spiritual growth together a priority. You might want to include items such as keeping "dates," working through HomeBuilders Projects, participating in the study group, and encouraging each other.

After writing your pledge, sign it to signify your commitment.

Personal Pledge

SIGNATURES

DATE

5. Pray together, asking God to guide you to achieve new levels of spiritual growth in your marriage.

Remember to bring your calendar to the next session so you can Make a Date.

The Power of Prayer in Marriage

Prayer promotes growth in your relationships with God and with your spouse.

W A R M • U P   15   M I N U T E S

Practiced Prayer

Whether or not you grew up in a "Christian" home, you learned about prayer as you observed the attitudes and practices of family, friends, church members, or even characters in television shows and movies.

For fun, recite aloud any memorized prayers you still remember.

- What do you remember about your concept of prayer as a child?
- How has your concept of prayer changed since you were a child? Why?

Project Report

Share one thing you learned from the HomeBuilders Project from last session.

BLUEPRINTS   6 0   M I N U T E S

Barriers to Prayer

If you have a large group, form smaller groups of about six people to answer the Blueprints questions. Unless otherwise noted, answer the questions in your subgroup. After finishing each section, take time for subgroups to share their answers with the whole group.

It's important to examine barriers to prayer so that couples can identify what keeps them from praying more.

1. What do you think keeps people from praying more than they do?

2. Why do you think many Christian couples spend little time together in prayer?

Benefits of Prayer

3. What does God's Word say about how prayer can help you grow in your relationship with God? Have each couple take one of the following passages. (It's OK for more than one couple to have the same passage or for a couple to take more than one passage depending on the number in your group.)

- 2 Chronicles 7:14
- Matthew 6:6
- Matthew 26:41
- Philippians 4:6-7
- James 1:5
- James 5:16

Read your Scripture together and discuss the benefit of prayer revealed in your passage. Then share your passage and what you discovered with the group.

4. If you've ever experienced one of the truths of the previous verses, tell about that experience. How have you received God's wisdom or peace, or how have you experienced God's presence through prayer?

Basic Components of Prayer

Because prayer is talking with God, it's a wonderful way to develop your relationship with him. But many people know little about what to do as they pray.

The psalms are among the best known and loved writings of all literature. Many psalms are actually prayers, and from them we can learn about basic components of prayer.

Praise

The element of prayer that psalms are best known for is praise. Throughout the book of Psalms, David and other psalmists express their adoration of God.

5. Read Psalm 96:1-10. What does it mean to praise God? If a person were to consistently spend significant time praising God, how would that affect the way that person looks at problems he or she faces?

6. What is something you can praise God for right now? Tell your group about it.

Confession

In Psalm 51, one of the greatest examples of confession in the Bible, David confesses his sins of committing adultery with Bathsheba and sending her husband off to be killed in battle.

7. Read Psalm 51:1-13. What things was David seeking in this confession? What was the attitude behind his confession?

8. Read 1 John 1:9. What does God promise to do when we confess sin? Why is confession important in our relationship with God?

Supplication

Psalm 34 is often read and quoted to encourage us to bring our needs and desires to God in prayer.

9. Read Psalm 34:4-18. Quietly reflect on the effect prayer can have in a person's life. After a few minutes, share your thoughts with your group.

10. Read Matthew 7:7-11. How should this passage affect our attitudes about making requests to God?

Praying Together

Answer questions 11 and 12 with your spouse. After answering, you may want to share an appropriate insight or discovery with the group.

11. Read Matthew 18:19-20. How do these verses relate to praying together as a couple? How would your marriage benefit if you were to pray together more consistently?

12. Identify two or three things that make praying together difficult for you. What steps can you take to resolve one of these difficulties?

HomeBuilders Principle:
Praying together affirms your unified dependence on God and helps produce the cleansing, humility, and unity essential to continued spiritual growth in marriage.

WRAP · UP 15 MINUTES

Now it's time to practice what you've been learning. Turn to your spouse and talk about one need in your lives right now—it could be something you'd like to see God accomplish in the lives of your children, in your marriage, in your careers, or in any other part of your lives. Take turns praying simple one- or two-sentence prayers. Spend a few minutes praising God, confessing sins as you need to, and telling God about your needs and the needs of others.

Make a Date

Make a date with your spouse to meet before the next session to complete the HomeBuilders Project. At the next session, your leader will ask you to share one thing from this experience.

DATE

TIME

LOCATION

As a Couple [5 minutes]

Begin by sharing with each other

- the cutest or most humorous thing you remember praying for in your childhood or youth, or

- the cutest or most humorous thing you've heard a child pray for.

Individually [20 minutes]

1. What insight did you gain about prayer in marriage from this session?

2. How well do you feel you and your spouse do at praying together? What is one thing you could do to improve in this area?

3. When you pray, on which of the three components (praise, confession, supplication) do you spend the most time? On which do you spend the least amount of time?

4. Using Psalm 96 as a guide, spend time praising God for who he is and what he has done in your life. Write a list of specific things to praise God for.

5. Read 1 John 1:9. Now spend a few moments confessing any sin that is blocking growth in your relationship with God. Then thank God for forgiving those sins.

6. What needs do you have or know about? List them as prayer requests, then pray through the list.

Interact as a Couple [35 minutes]
1. Share with each other the insights of your individual time.

2. What do you see as the value of praying together?

3. Choose a time and place for regular prayer together.

4. One tool that can help make prayer meaningful and significant in your life is a **Prayer Journal**. In it you enter particular prayer needs and dates, leaving some space so that later you can record what happened after you prayed.

As part of this study, keep a **Prayer Journal** for the next few weeks. Doing this will give you a measurable way of seeing God at work in your lives. Few experiences are more exciting!

You can use the "Prayer Journal" pages in the back of your books to list and date things you'd like to begin praying for as a couple.

5. Following the outline of praise, confession, and supplication, spend a few minutes in prayer together.

Remember to bring your calendar to the next session so you can Make a Date.

The Guidebook for Growth

The greatest Book ever written is God's gift to help you grow closer to him and to your spouse.

W A R M • U P   15 M I N U T E S

I Love to Tell the Story

Begin by sharing one of the following with the group:

- a favorite Bible story from your childhood and why it's a favorite,

- a Bible passage that has been particularly meaningful in your life or in your marriage, or

- your thoughts about the Bible's relevance to your life.

Project Report

Share one thing you learned from the HomeBuilders Project from last session.

The Book of Books

This brief essay by Henry Van Dyke expresses how the Bible is a treasure to all.

Born in the East and clothed in Oriental form and imagery, the Bible walks the ways of all the world with familiar feet, and enters land after land to find its own everywhere. It has learned to speak in hundreds of languages to the heart of man. It comes into the palace to tell the monarch that he is a servant of the Most High, and into the cottage to assure the peasant that he is a son of God. Children listen to its stories with wonder and delight and wise men ponder them as parables of life. It has a word of peace for the time of peril, a word of comfort for the time of calamity, a word of light for the hour of darkness. Its oracles are repeated in the assembly of the people, and its counsels whispered in the ear of the lonely.

The wicked and the proud tremble at its warnings, but to the wounded and the penitent it has a mother's voice. The wilderness and the solitary place have been made glad by it, and the fire on the hearth has lit the reading of its well-worn pages. It has woven itself into our dearest dreams; so that love, friendship, sympathy and devotion, memory and hope put on the beautiful garments of its treasured speech, breathing of frankincense and myrrh.

1. What thoughts about the Bible does this essay inspire in you? From your experience, what benefits have you gained from reading and studying the Bible?

If you have a large group, form smaller groups of about six people to answer the Blueprints questions. Unless otherwise noted, answer the questions in your subgroup. After finishing each section, take time for subgroups to share their answers with the whole group.

2. Read Psalm 119:160. Why is it so important in today's culture to know that God's Word presents absolute, everlasting truth?

> **HomeBuilders Principle:**
> *The Bible gives you a solid foundation for making moral and ethical decisions in your marriage.*

Our Personal Treasure

3. Read Psalm 19:7-11. How can God's Word revive the soul?

4. Read Psalm 119:49-50. How does the Bible comfort you in difficult times?

5. Read Psalm 119:114. How does the Word of God give you hope?

6. What obstacles keep you from studying the Bible consistently as an individual? as a couple?

HomeBuilders Principle:
If you value knowing the Bible and applying it to your life, you will discover the spiritual food your souls need to survive.

Step-by-Step Study

7. If you have studied the Bible together as a couple, how have you done it? What has worked for you?

8. If you were to study the Bible with your spouse on a regular basis, what effect do you think this would have on your marriage relationship?

A Three-Step Approach to Bible Study

- **Step One:** *What does it say?* Observe the text and the word relationships of the passage you're studying. Seek to understand what the passage is saying.

- **Step Two:** *What does it mean?* Dig into the passage. Ask questions such as, "Why did the author say this? What message was the author trying to get across?"

- **Step Three:** *What does it mean to me?* Apply to your life what you have learned. Determine what difference this truth can and will make in your life right now.

---

9. Why is Bible application important to your growth both as an individual and as a couple?

10. Using the three-step approach outlined above, do a brief Bible study with your spouse on Philippians 4:6-7. Read the passage twice, slowly and carefully. Then proceed with the three steps:

Do question 10 with your spouse.
Note: Be sure to work through these steps in an attitude of prayer, asking God to help you understand and apply his Word.

Step One: *What does it say?*

- What is the main idea of this passage?

- What are some of the key words?

Step Two: *What does it mean?*

- What does it mean to "not be anxious about anything"?

- What does it mean to pray about everything?

- How does the peace of God transcend all under-standing?

Step Three: *What does it mean to me?*

- How does praying to God give you this peace? Have you ever experienced God's peace after you prayed about a situation you were anxious about? Tell about the experience, if you can.

- What are some situations that you're anxious about right now? What does this passage say you should do about your anxiety? Spend a few minutes in prayer right now about these situations, and ask for God's guidance and peace.

When you have finished this study as a couple, share some of your observations with the group.

HomeBuilders Principle:
Growing together in Christ as a couple requires regular study of God's Word.

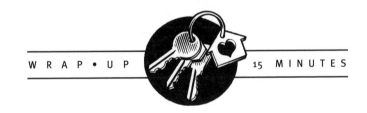

W R A P • U P   15   M I N U T E S

Discuss the following questions as a whole group, giving everyone a chance to respond.

- Tell about a time you tried to put something

complicated together without looking at the instructions. How did it turn out?

- How is putting something together without looking at the instructions like trying to build a healthy marriage without studying the Bible?

- How can you overcome obstacles to studying the Bible together as a couple? Brainstorm a list of things you may want to try.

For Extra Impact

It's Puzzling: Use this exercise as a fun way to illustrate the power of direction in our lives.

As a group spend some time trying to put together a puzzle without seeing the box top. After you've worked at this for a while, discuss these questions:

- How is putting a puzzle together without the picture like trying to follow God in your marriage without studying the Bible?

- What are some things you can do to better ensure that studying the Bible becomes a habit in your life?

Make a Date

Make a date with your spouse to meet before the next session to complete the HomeBuilders Project. At the next session, your leader will ask you to share one thing from this experience.

DATE

TIME

LOCATION

HOMEBUILDERS PROJECT   6 o   M I N U T E S

As a Couple [10 minutes]

As you begin, share with each other

- the book (other than the Bible) that has had the greatest influence on your life and why,

- the person who has had the greatest influence on your life and why, and

- the influence the Bible has had on your life and why.

Individually [20 minutes]

1. What is one insight or discovery you gained from this session?

2. When has the Bible made a significant difference in your life?

3. What would be helpful to you in studying the Bible regularly as an individual and as a couple?

4. What needs could the Bible help you with right now?

5. What is currently preventing you from spending time in God's Word individually? as a couple?

Interact as a Couple* [30 minutes]*

1. Share the work you completed in the individual time. Listen nonjudgmentally, being sensitive for ways you can help and encourage your spouse to spend time in the Word.

2. Come up with a plan for reading and studying the Bible together regularly. There are numerous approaches to studying the Bible; here are just a few to get you started.

Reading Programs

- Read through the Bible in a year. Several programs are available to help you do this.
- Read a chapter of the Gospel of John each day. It's probably the best single presentation of the gospel in the Bible.
- Choose a book of the Bible to read, and each day read in it until you find something that really hits you. You may also want to keep a journal, writing down things that speak to you.

Study Programs

- Explore different books of the Bible. Pick a book, preferably a short one to start with, and read through it two or three times noting themes and favorite verses. Use the three steps described in the Blueprints section.

- Examine the lives and experiences of people in the Bible. Choose a character—Joseph, Daniel, Esther, Peter, or any character you relate to—and find all the passages in which this character is mentioned. Look for clues to the person's strengths, weaknesses, and motivations. Seek to apply this person's experiences to your own life.
- Study key words in the Bible. Choose a word such as "peace" or "humility" and, using a Bible concordance, look up verses in which the word appears.

3. Commit together to a regular schedule of studying the Bible as a couple.

4. Pray for current needs and concerns together, and commit your plans and purposes to the Lord. Ask God to help you succeed in studying the Bible together as you seek to grow together in Christ.

Remember to bring your calendar to the next session so you can Make a Date.

Growing Together Through the Holy Spirit

When you draw upon the Holy Spirit's power, you will experience growth in your life and in your marriage relationship.

W A R M • U P   15   M I N U T E S

Invisible Power

Line up side by side with everyone holding an uninflated balloon and facing in the same direction. When your leader gives the signal, throw your balloon as far out in front of you as you can.

Retrieve your balloon and inflate it. Don't tie it off, but hold the opening closed so that the air doesn't escape. Again, line up with the other group members, aim your balloon out in front of you, and at your leader's signal let it go. After the confusion and laughter, pick up your balloon and sit down to discuss the following questions:

- Which time did the balloon travel a greater over-all distance?

- Which time did the balloon end up somewhere unexpected?

- What made the difference in the way the balloon traveled?

- Which time was more fun?

- How might this activity be like God working in a person's life through the power of the Holy Spirit?

- In general, how well do you think people under-stand the ministry of the Holy Spirit? When you think of the Holy Spirit and how the Spirit works in the lives of Christians what comes to your mind?

Project Report

Share one thing you learned from the HomeBuilders Project from last session.

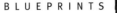

Power Shortage

Case Study

When Dan and Nancy became Christians two years ago, their lives changed dramatically. They began to study the Bible regularly, getting up early every morning to make sure they could read God's Word and pray together before their busy day began.

Dan and Nancy attend church every Sunday morning with bright smiles on their faces. Nancy sings in the choir, and they both attend Sunday school. Dan has even gone on overnight camping trips with the junior high group a couple of times.

Though Dan and Nancy appear to be model young believers, lately they have confessed to frustration in their spiritual lives. The joy is fading. They feel so apprehensive about telling their friends and neighbors about Jesus that they just don't say anything. And then they feel guilty. At times it seems as if they're just going through the motions with all these Christian activities, and the Christian life is beginning to get boring. For all their efforts, they don't really feel close to God, and they don't feel his presence and power.

1. What may be wrong in Dan and Nancy's relationship with God?

> If you have a large group, form smaller groups of about six people to answer the Blueprints questions. Unless otherwise noted, answer the questions in your subgroup. After finishing each section, take time for subgroups to share their answers with the whole group.

2. Read Ephesians 3:16-19. How might this passage relate to Dan and Nancy's problem? How does this passage relate to your experience of the Christian life?

The Holy Spirit in Us

3. Read 2 Peter 1:3. What could you as a couple be missing if you try to live the Christian life in your own power?

For question 4, you may want each couple to examine one or more passages and then report their findings to the group.

4. What do the following passages say about your relationship with the Holy Spirit?

• John 14:16-17

• John 16:13-15

• Acts 1:8

• Romans 8:26-27

• 2 Timothy 1:14

God's Fruit in Our Lives

5. Read Galatians 5:19-21. How have you seen "the acts of the sinful nature" cause problems in your marriage?

Answer questions 5 and 6 with your spouse. After answering, you may want to share an appropriate insight or discovery with the group.

6. Now read Galatians 5:22-23. What are the results of living in the power of the Spirit? Which of these "fruit of the Spirit" characteristics do you think your spouse would like to see more of in your life, and how would that fruitfulness help your marriage?

Living by the Holy Spirit

7. Read Galatians 5:16-18. What does it mean to "live by the Spirit"? How can you do that in your marriage?

8. Read 1 John 1:5-10. Why is confession of our sins necessary preparation for the Holy Spirit to work in us?

9. Read Romans 12:1-2. What does this passage suggest we do in response to God's mercy? How does this relate to living by the Holy Spirit?

10. Read 1 John 5:14-15. What will God do if you ask him to take control of your life through the Holy Spirit?

11. Read Romans 15:13. What difference will it make to you and your spouse if you turn your lives over to God's control?

12. If both marriage partners daily seek to live by the Holy Spirit, what traits would you expect that marriage to exhibit?

Take a few moments to allow volunteers to share how
the Holy Spirit has made a difference in their lives
and in their marriages.

After a few have shared, move to a time of quiet personal reflection and prayer.

- If you feel that you're already living consistently by
  the Holy Spirit, pray silently for others in your group
  who might be struggling with giving God control.

- If you would like the power of the Holy Spirit in your
  life and your marriage, give God control of your life.
  Confess your sins, and let the Holy Spirit take over.
  To live consistently in the power of the Holy Spirit,
  you need to make certain that you are living under
  God's control *daily*. **Silently offer the following
  prayer if it reflects the desire of your heart:**

*Dear God, I need you. I acknowledge that I have been in
control of my life and that I have sinned against you. I ask
for your forgiveness and thank you that you have forgiven
my sins through Christ's death on the cross for me. I now
ask you to again take control of my life. Empower and*

guide me through your Holy Spirit. As an expression of my faith, I now thank you for guiding my life through the Holy Spirit. I pray this in Jesus' name, amen.

For more information about how to live by the Holy Spirit, be sure to read "Our Problems, God's Answers" in the back of this book.

Make a Date

Make a date with your spouse to meet before the next session to complete the HomeBuilders Project. At the next session, your leader will ask you to share one thing from this experience.

DATE

TIME

LOCATION

HOMEBUILDERS PROJECT   6 0   M I N U T E S

As a Couple [5 minutes]

Talk together about the following questions:

- In our marriage, have we been living by the Holy Spirit like the way

  a. a goldfish in its tank responds to its owner's instructions?

  b. a cat responds to its caretaker's requests?

  c. a dog responds to its master's commands?

  d. a horse responds to the person holding its reins?

- What relationship in these examples from nature best parallels how God wants us to respond to him?

Individually [20 minutes]

1. From this session, explain one insight you gained about the role of the Holy Spirit in your marriage.

2. How would your marriage be different if both you and your spouse truly lived by the Holy Spirit?

3. In what areas of your life do you most need God's guidance and power?

4. Take a few minutes to look again at Galatians 5:16-23. As you look at your life during the last few months, would you say you've been living mostly by the desires of the sinful nature or by the Spirit? How would you characterize your resulting lifestyle?

5. What is one practical way your spouse can encourage you to "live by the Spirit"?

6. It's important to walk in the Spirit on a daily basis. The process of walking in the Spirit is one of continually yielding to God's control in your life. Bill Bright, founder of Campus Crusade for Christ, calls this process "spiritual breathing":

Exhale: Confess, according to 1 John 1:9, the sin that has broken your stride.

Inhale: Pray that the Holy Spirit will once again take control of your life, and thank God for the renewal of his powerful presence in your life.

What is one recent, specific situation at home, at work, or in your car in which it would have been good for you to apply this principle?

Interact as a Couple [35 minutes]

1. Share with each other your responses and insights from the individual time.

2. Read Ephesians 5:15-21 to each other. While your spouse reads, think about how these commands can make a difference in your life together. Then brainstorm ways you can incorporate some of these commands into your lives.

3. What actions will you take to assure that both of you daily seek and follow the Holy Spirit's leading in your lives?

4. In your **Prayer Journal** in the back of this book, update any answers to prayer and add further requests. Finish by praying through your **Prayer Journal** together and committing your plans and purposes to the Lord. Pray that God will help you remain faithful in living daily by the Holy Spirit.

Remember to bring your calendar to the next session so you can Make a Date.

Following Jesus

Faithfully following Jesus will help you grow together
in Christ and in your marriage.

W A R M • U P   15   M I N U T E S

Reflections

Stand facing your spouse. For the start of this activity,
each wife will be a "reflectee," and each husband a
"reflector." Wives are to make any motions or facial
expressions they want to, and husbands are to move
as if they were the mirror reflections of their wives.
After about thirty seconds, switch roles. After another
thirty seconds, sit down to discuss the following questions with the whole group.

- What was it like trying to follow your spouse's
  actions?

- What was most important to successful following?

- How is this like following Jesus as Christians?

- How is it different?

Project Report

Share one thing you learned from the HomeBuilders Project from last session.

BLUEPRINTS   60 MINUTES

While living on earth, Jesus called men and women to follow him—to become "learners" or disciples. God still calls men and women to follow him today.

If you have a large group, form smaller groups of about six people to answer the Blueprints questions. Unless otherwise noted, answer the questions in your subgroup. After finishing each section, take time for subgroups to share their answers with the whole group.

Following Christ

1. Read 2 Corinthians 3:18. What does it mean to become like Christ?

2. Another aspect of following Christ was revealed when Jesus chose his first disciples. Read Matthew 4:18-22, and imagine yourself in this passage. What do you think was difficult about their decision to follow Christ?

3. What did they give up? What did they gain?

4. Whom do you know who seems to have a fervent desire to serve Christ wholeheartedly? What sets that person apart from other Christians?

5. In what way are you called to follow Christ today?

HomeBuilders Principle:
God wants you to follow him wholeheartedly by becoming like Christ and commiting your life completely to him.

The Cost of Following Christ

6. Read what Jesus told his disciples in Matthew 10:37-39. Now read it again. What hits you hardest from this passage?

7. What sacrifices have you made in your life to follow Jesus?

8. What does this passage say to the church today? What are examples of "crosses" Jesus might expect us to take up?

Answer questions 9 and 10 with your spouse. After answering, you may want to share an appropriate insight or discovery with the group.

9. When in your marriage have you really sought to follow God? When have you definitely followed your own desires?

10. How would your relationship change if you fully applied Matthew 10:37-39 in your marriage?

The Benefits of Discipleship

11. Have each couple look up one or two of the following passages. Read your passage, and discuss with your spouse what it says about the benefits of following Jesus.

- Matthew 11:28-30

- Luke 18:28-30

- John 8:31-32

- John 10:9-10

- Ephesians 3:20-21

Now take turns sharing with the group your passage and insights into the benefits of following Jesus.

12. What specific actions are involved in daily following God? How can these draw you together as a couple?

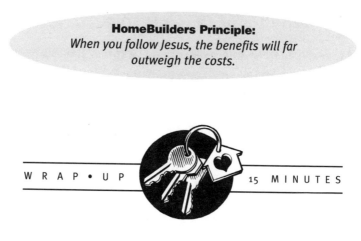

HomeBuilders Principle:
When you follow Jesus, the benefits will far outweigh the costs.

W R A P • U P   15 M I N U T E S

Now it's time to make following God real in your life. Turn to your spouse and talk about specific ways that you as individuals and as a couple can more fully follow God

- at home,

- at church,

- at work, and

- in your neighborhood.

Commit to doing at least one of these things as a couple sometime before your next group meeting. Share with the rest of the group what you plan to do.

For Extra Impact

As a demonstration of following God, plan a community service project with your group. You might work with a homeless shelter, a food bank, a home-repair agency, or a church ministry. Begin planning this week, solidify your plans by next week, and try to do the project within a week or two after that. Be sure to talk about the experience afterward, and consider additional projects that God might want you involved in.

Make a Date

Make a date with your spouse to meet before the next session to complete the HomeBuilders Project. At the next session, your leader will ask you to share one thing from this experience.

DATE

TIME

LOCATION

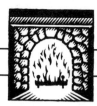

As a Couple [10 minutes]

Think for a moment about the following questions, then talk about your responses.

- Apart from God, who or what do you follow in varying degrees? You might think of a sports team, a television show, an actor or actress, an athlete, an automobile, a musician, or the stock market.

- Compare your following the person or thing to following God.

Individually [20 minutes]

1. From this session, explain one insight about following God that has had the most impact on you.

2. Read John 13:34-35. Why do Christians who demonstrate love stand out in today's culture?

3. When have you stood up for Christ or showed love in a way that demonstrated to others how much you love God?

4. Why is it sometimes difficult to follow Jesus in this way?

5. How has God blessed you as you've sought to follow him?

6. What things in your life sometimes keep you from following God? What can you do about these things?

Interact as a Couple [30 minutes]

1. Share your answers from the individual time.

2. Decide on three action steps you can take to follow Christ more fully as a couple. List your steps here:

3. Update your **Prayer Journal** in the back of this book, noting any answers to prayer or additional requests. Finish by praying through your journal, and also committing your plans and purposes to the Lord. Look to God to enable you to achieve success in the area of growing together in Christ.

4. Read the following prayer silently, and consider whether you can pray it as the honest sharing of your heart with God. If so, pray it aloud together.

Dear God, Thank you for drawing me to follow you. With the Holy Spirit as my guide and helper, I seek to follow you in every part of my life. Thank you for forgiving me when I fall short of that goal and for helping me get my focus back on you. Help me to show love to others so that the world will see that I'm your disciple. Help both of us draw closer together in our marriage as we draw closer to you. In Jesus' name, amen.

Remember to bring your calendar to the next session so you can Make a Date.

Making Disciples

If you're growing together as a couple, you will reproduce yourselves spiritually and make an impact for God on generations to come.

W A R M • U P   15   M I N U T E S

Positive Impact

- Share how this group has made an impact on your spiritual growth as a couple through the course of this study.

- Think of someone else who has made an important contribution to your Christian life. What did this person do to make such an impact?

- How did this person "reproduce" himself or herself in you?

For Extra Impact

After the first question in "Positive Impact," make something out of modeling dough or clay that represents something someone has helped develop in your life—a certain character trait or spiritual discipline, for example. Share what you made with the rest of the group. Then divide your clay in half, and make two smaller versions of the same item. Discuss the following questions:

- How was this activity like reproducing yourself as a Christian?
- How was it different?
- What insights from this activity have you gained about making disciples?

Project Report

Share one thing you learned from the HomeBuilders Project from last session.

BLUEPRINTS   60 MINUTES

As a result of abiding in Christ, we will bear fruit: We

will reproduce ourselves spiritually by helping others become disciples of Jesus.

God Can Use You!

1. Read Matthew 4:18-20. In our last session we looked at this passage to discover what it means to follow Jesus. Now discuss the following question: What does it mean to become "fishers of men"?

If you have a large group, form smaller groups of about six people to answer the Blueprints questions. Unless otherwise noted, answer the questions in your subgroup. After finishing each section, take time for subgroups to share their answers with the whole group.

2. Read the following Bible passages, and answer these questions: What types of people does God tend to use to accomplish his purposes on earth? How are these people like you? unlike you? (You might have each couple look up one or two of the passages and then share their answers.)

• Exodus 4:10-12

• Isaiah 6:5-8

- Amos 7:14-15

- Matthew 4:18

- Luke 5:27

3. What did these people have to offer God?

HomeBuilders Principle:
God can use you if you let him.

Telling Others

4. Read Matthew 9:36-37. What do you think Jesus meant when he said "the harvest is plentiful but the workers are few"? How true are his words today?

5. Why do you think many Christians are silent about their faith outside the walls of their churches and homes? What can be done about that? Whose responsibility is it to do something?

6. According to John 16:7-11, who is ultimately responsible for convincing men and women that they need Christ? How does that knowledge affect the way you feel about sharing your faith?

7. Read Matthew 28:19-20. What is your responsibility in making disciples?

The Impact of Disciple Making

8. Share an experience in which God gave you an opportunity to tell someone about your faith. How did that experience affect that person? How did it affect you?

9. Read 2 Timothy 2:2. In what ways have you seen God use you and your spouse together to help others grow in their faith? What other opportunities do you see available to you now?

Your Most Important Disciples

10. Read 2 Timothy 3:14-16. How do you think Timothy's experience as a child shaped him for his future ministry?

11. If you have children, why are they your most important disciples? If you don't have children, who are the people you most want to see become growing Christians? In either case, what kinds of things have you done to lead your most important disciples toward a growing faith in Jesus?

Answer questions 11 and 12 with your spouse. After answering, you may want to share an appropriate insight or discovery with the group.

12. What's one step you need to take to make more of a spiritual impact on these most important disciples?

WRAP • UP   15 MINUTES

As you come to the end of this study, take some time as a group to reflect on what you have experienced by answering these questions.

- What has this group meant to you during the course of this study? Be specific.

- What is the most valuable thing you discovered or learned?

- What would you like to see happen next for this group?

- How have you been changed or challenged?

For Extra Impact

Using a pen or pencil, trace around your hand onto
paper. Then discuss these questions:

- How does drawing your hand illustrate duplicating
  yourself as you seek to make disciples for Jesus?

- What things might you *not* want to see duplicated
  in someone else?

- Now write on each finger of your drawing something you feel you should change in your life to
  become a better disciple maker. Take your paper
  home, and post it where it will remind you of
  what you want to improve in your relationship
  with God and others.

Make a Date

Make a date with your spouse to meet in the next few
days to complete the last HomeBuilders Project of
this study.

DATE

TIME

LOCATION

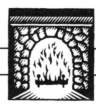

As a Couple [10 minutes]

Begin by e-mailing, calling on the phone, or writing a letter to someone who has influenced both of you spiritually. Thank that person for the impact he or she has had on your life.

Individually [20 minutes]

1. From this session, explain one insight about making disciples that has had the most impact on you.

2. What can you do to get more involved in making disciples?

3. Identify areas in which you feel you need the most help in being well-prepared to make disciples:

__ Introducing Christ into a conversation

__ Sharing your faith story

__ Explaining the gospel

__ Guiding your friend to make a faith commitment

__ Other:_____

4. Determine what you can do to get the help you need. Write some ideas here.

5. Choose what you will commit to doing in reaching out to others to begin making disciples. Write that here.

6. Personally make your commitment to God in prayer.

Interact as a Couple [30 minutes]

1. Share with each other what you wrote down and committed to during the individual time.

2. What is keeping you as a couple from being used

by God to influence others for Christ? What steps should you take to correct this situation?

3. Write down the names of at least four people you would like to see make a faith commitment to Christ or grow in their faith.

4. Discuss the needs you see in the lives of these people and things you have in common that might help you develop relationships with them. Determine what you will do as a couple this week to begin reaching out to one of the individuals or couples on your list.

5. Together, pray by name for the people you listed, alternating in offering these prayers. Specifically ask God to use you in sharing Jesus with each person.

Where Do You Go From Here?

It is our prayer that you have benefited greatly from this study in the HomeBuilders Couples Series. We hope that your marriage will continue to grow as you both submit your lives to Jesus Christ and build according to his blueprints.

We also hope that you will begin reaching out to strengthen other marriages in your community and local church. Your church needs couples like you who are committed to building Christian marriages. A favorite World War II story illustrates this point very clearly.

The year was 1940. The French Army had just collapsed under Hitler's onslaught. The Dutch had folded, overwhelmed by the Nazi regime. The Belgians had surrendered. And the British Army was trapped on the coast of France in the channel port of Dunkirk.

Two hundred and twenty thousand of Britain's finest young men seemed doomed to die, turning the English Channel red with their blood. The Fuehrer's troops, only miles away in the hills of France, didn't realize how close to victory they actually were.

Any rescue seemed feeble and futile in the time remaining. A "thin" British Navy—"the professionals"—told King George VI that at best they could save 17,000 troops. The House of Commons was warned to prepare for "hard and heavy tidings."

Politicians were paralyzed. The king was powerless. And the Allies could only watch as spectators from a distance. Then as the doom of the British Army seemed imminent, a strange fleet appeared on the horizon of the English Channel—the wildest assortment of boats perhaps ever assembled in history. Trawlers, tugs, scows, fishing sloops, lifeboats, pleasure craft, smacks and coasters, sailboats, even the London fire-brigade flotilla. *Each ship was manned by civilian volunteers—English fathers sailing to rescue Britain's exhausted, bleeding sons.*

William Manchester writes in his epic novel, *The Last Lion*, that even today what happened in 1940 in less than twenty-four hours seems like a miracle—not only were all of the British soldiers rescued, but 118,000 other Allied troops as well.

Today the Christian home is much like those troops at Dunkirk. Pressured, trapped, and demoralized, it needs help. Your help. The Christian community may be much like England—we stand waiting for politicians, professionals, even for our pastors to step in and save the family. But the problem is much larger than all of those combined can solve.

With the highest divorce rate of any nation on earth, we need an all-out effort by men and women "sailing" to rescue the exhausted and wounded family casualties. We need an outreach effort by common couples with faith in an uncommon God. For too long, married couples within the church have abdicated the privilege and responsibility of influencing others to those in full-time vocational ministry.

Possibly this study has indeed been used to "light the torch" of your spiritual lives. Perhaps it was already burning, and this provided more fuel. Regardless, may we challenge you to invest your lives in others?

You and other couples around the world can team together to build thousands of marriages and families. By starting a HomeBuilders group, you will not only strengthen other marriages; you will also see your marriage grow as you share these principles with others.

Will You Join Us in "Touching Lives...Changing Families"?

The following are some practical ways you can make a difference in families today:

1. Gather a group of four to eight couples, and lead them through the six sessions of this HomeBuilders study, *Growing Together in Christ.* (Why not consider challenging others in your church or community to form additional HomeBuilders groups?)

2. Commit to continue marriage building by doing another course in the HomeBuilders Couples Series.

3. An excellent outreach tool is the film *"JESUS,"* which is available on video. For more information, contact FamilyLife at 1-800-FL-TODAY.

4. Host a dinner party. Invite families from your neighborhood to your home, and as a couple share your faith in Christ.

5. Reach out and share the love of Christ with neighborhood children.

6. If you have attended the FamilyLife Marriage Conference, why not offer to assist your pastor in counseling couples engaged to be married, using the material you received?

For more information about any of the above ministry opportunities, contact your local church, or write:

FamilyLife
P.O. Box 8220
Little Rock, AR 72221-8220
1-800-FL-TODAY
www.familylife.com

Our Problems, God's Answers

•

Every couple eventually has to deal with problems in marriage. Communication problems. Money problems. Difficulties with sexual intimacy. These issues are important to cultivating a strong, loving relationship with your spouse. The HomeBuilders Couples Series is designed to help you strengthen your marriage in many of these critical areas.

Part One: The Big Problem

One basic problem is at the heart of every other problem in every marriage, and it's a problem we can't help you fix. No matter how hard you try, this is one problem that is too big for you to deal with on your own.

The problem is separation from God. If you want to experience marriage the way it was designed to be, you need a vital relationship with the God who created you and offers you the power to live a life of joy and purpose.

And what separates us from God is one more problem—sin. Most of us have assumed throughout our lives that the term "sin" refers to a list of bad habits that everyone agrees are wrong. We try to deal with our sin problem by working hard to become better people. We read books to learn how to control our anger, or we resolve to stop cheating on our taxes.

But in our hearts, we know our sin problem runs much deeper than a list of bad habits. All of us have rebelled against God. We have ignored him and have decided to run our own lives in a way that makes sense to us. The Bible says that the God who created us wants us to follow his plan for our lives, not our own. But because of our sin problem, we think our ideas and plans are better than his.

- *"For all have sinned and fall short of the glory of God"* (Romans 3:23).

What does it mean to "fall short of the glory of God"? It means that none of us has trusted and treasured God the way we should. We have sought to satisfy ourselves with other things and have treated those things as more valuable than God. We have gone our own way. According to the Bible, we have to pay a penalty for our sin. We cannot simply do things the way we choose and hope it will all be OK with God. Following our own plan leads to our destruction.

- *"There is a way that seems right to a man, but in the end it leads to death"* (Proverbs 14:12).

- *"For the wages of sin is death"* (Romans 6:23a).

The penalty for sin is that we are forever separated from God's love. God is holy, and we are sinful. No matter how hard we try, we cannot come up with some plan, like living a good life or even trying to do what the Bible says, and hope that we can avoid the penalty.

God's Solution to Sin

Thankfully God has a way to solve our dilemma. He became a man through the person of Jesus Christ. He lived a holy life, in perfect obedience to God's plan. He also willingly died on a cross to pay our penalty for sin. Then he proved that he is more powerful than sin or death by rising from the dead. He alone has the power to overrule the penalty for our sin.

- *"Jesus answered, 'I am the way and the truth and the life. No one comes to the Father except through me'"* (John 14:6).

- *"But God demonstrates his own love for us in this: While we were still sinners, Christ died for us"* (Romans 5:8).

- *"Christ died for our sins...he was buried...he was raised on the third day according to the Scriptures...he appeared to Peter, and then to the Twelve. After that, he appeared to more than five hundred"* (1 Corinthians 15:3-6).

- *"For the wages of sin is death, but the gift of God is eternal life in Christ Jesus our Lord"* (Romans 6:23).

The death of Jesus has fixed our sin problem. He has bridged the gap between God and us. He is calling all of us to come to him and to give up our own flawed plan for how to run our lives. He wants us to trust God and his plan.

Accepting God's Solution

If you agree that you are separated from God, he is calling you to confess your sins. All of us have made messes of our lives because we have stubbornly preferred our ideas and plans over his. As a result, we deserve to be cut off from God's love and his care for us. But God has promised that if we will agree that we have rebelled against his plan for us and have messed up our lives, he will forgive us and will fix our sin problem.

- *"Yet to all who received him, to those who believed in his name, he gave the right to become children of God"* (John 1:12).

- *"For it is by grace you have been saved, through faith—and this not from yourselves, it is the gift of*

God—not by works, so that no one can boast" (Ephesians 2:8-9).

When the Bible talks about receiving Christ, it means we acknowledge that we are sinners and that we can't fix the problem ourselves. It means we turn away from our sin. And it means we trust Christ to forgive our sins and to make us the kind of people he wants us to be. It's not enough to just intellectually believe that Christ is the Son of God. We must trust in him and his plan for our lives by faith, as an act of the will.

Are things right between you and God, with him and his plan at the center of your life? Or is life spinning out of control as you seek to make your way on your own?

You can decide today to make a change. You can turn to Christ and allow him to transform your life. All you need to do is to talk to him and tell him what is stirring in your mind and in your heart. If you've never done this before, consider taking the steps listed here:

- Do you agree that you need God? Tell God.

- Have you made a mess of your life by following your own plan? Tell God.

- Do you want God to forgive you? Tell God.

- Do you believe that Jesus' death on the cross and his resurrection from the dead gave him the power to fix your sin problem and to grant you the free gift of eternal life? Tell God.

- Are you ready to acknowledge that God's plan for your life is better than any plan you could come up with? Tell God.

- Do you agree that God has the right to be the Lord and master of your life? Tell God.

"Seek the Lord while he may be found;
call on him while he is near"
(Isaiah 55:6).

Following is a suggested prayer:

Lord Jesus, I need you. Thank you for dying on the
cross for my sins. I receive you as my Savior and Lord.
Thank you for forgiving my sins and giving me eternal
life. Make me the kind of person you want me to be.

Does this prayer express the desire of your heart? If it does,
pray it right now, and Christ will come into your life, as he
promised.

Part Two: Living the Christian Life

For a person who is a follower of Christ—a Christian—the
penalty for sin is paid in full. But the effect of sin continues
throughout our lives.

- *"If we claim to be without sin, we deceive ourselves*
  and the truth is not in us" (1 John 1:8).

- *"For what I do is not the good I want to do; no, the*
  evil I do not want to do—this I keep on doing"
  (Romans 7:19).

The effects of sin carry over into our marriages as well. Even
Christians struggle to maintain solid, God-honoring marriages.
Most couples eventually realize that they can't do it on their
own. But with God's help, they can succeed. The Holy Spirit
can have a huge impact in the marriages of Christians who live
constantly, moment by moment, under his gracious direction.

Self-Centered Christians

Many Christians struggle to live the Christian life in their own strength because they are not allowing God to control their lives. Their interests are self-directed, often resulting in failure and frustration.

- *"Brothers, I could not address you as spiritual but as worldly—mere infants in Christ. I gave you milk, not solid food, for you were not yet ready for it. Indeed, you are still not ready. You are still worldly. For since there is jealousy and quarreling among you, are you not worldly? Are you not acting like mere men?"* (1 Corinthians 3:1-3).

The self-centered Christian cannot experience the abundant and fruitful Christian life. Such people trust in their own efforts to live the Christian life: They are either uninformed about—or have forgotten—God's love, forgiveness, and power. This kind of Christian:

- has an up-and-down spiritual experience.

- cannot understand himself—he wants to do what is right, but cannot.

- fails to draw upon the power of the Holy Spirit to live the Christian life.

Some or all of the following traits may characterize the Christian who does not fully trust God:

Disobedience	Plagued by impure thoughts
Lack of love for God and others	Jealous
	Worrisome
Inconsistent prayer life	Easily discouraged, frustrated
Lack of desire for Bible study	Critical
Legalistic attitude	Lack of purpose

Note: The individual who professes to be a Christian but who continues to practice sin should realize that he may not be a Christian at all, according to 1 John 2:3; 3:6, 9; Ephesians 5:5.

Spirit-Centered Christians

When a Christian puts Christ on the throne of his life, he yields to God's control. This Christian's interests are directed by the Holy Spirit, resulting in harmony with God's plan.

- *"But the fruit of the Spirit is love, joy, peace, patience, kindness, goodness, faithfulness, gentleness and self-control. Against such things there is no law"* (Galatians 5:22, 23).

Jesus said,

- *"I have come that they may have life, and have it to the full"* (John 10:10b).

- *"I am the vine; you are the branches. If a man remains in me and I in him, he will bear much fruit; apart from me you can do nothing"* (John 15:5).

- *"But you will receive power when the Holy Spirit comes on you; and you will be my witnesses in Jerusalem, and in all Judea and Samaria, and to the ends of the earth"* (Acts 1:8).

The following traits result naturally from the Holy Spirit's work in our lives:

Christ centered	Love
Holy Spirit empowered	Joy
Motivated to tell others about Jesus	Peace
	Patience
Dedicated to prayer	Kindness
Student of God's Word	Goodness
Trusts God	Faithfulness
Obeys God	Gentleness
	Self-control

The degree to which these traits appear in a Christian's life and marriage depends upon the extent to which the Christian trusts the Lord with every detail of life, and upon that person's maturity in Christ. One who is only beginning to understand the ministry of the Holy Spirit should not be discouraged if he is not as fruitful as mature Christians who have known and experienced this truth for a longer period of time.

Giving God Control

Jesus promises his followers an abundant and fruitful life as they allow themselves to be directed and empowered by the Holy Spirit. As we give God control of our lives, Christ lives in and through us in the power of the Holy Spirit (John 15).

If you sincerely desire to be directed and empowered by God, you can turn your life over to the control of the Holy Spirit right now (Matthew 5:6; John 7:37-39).

First, confess your sins to God, agreeing with him that you want to turn from any past sinful patterns in your life. Thank God in faith that he has forgiven all of your sins because Christ died for you (Colossians 2:13-15; 1 John 1:9; 2:1-3; Hebrews 10:1-18).

Be sure to offer every area of your life to God (Romans 12:1, 2). Consider what areas you might rather keep to yourself, and be sure you're willing to give God control in those areas.

By faith, commit yourself to living according to the Holy Spirit's guidance and power.

- *Live by the Spirit:* *"So I say, live by the Spirit, and you will not gratify the desires of the sinful nature. For the sinful nature desires what is contrary to the Spirit, and the Spirit what is contrary to the sinful nature. They are in conflict with each other, so that you do not do what you want"* (Galatians 5:16-17).

- *Trust in God's Promise:* *"This is the confidence we have in approaching God: that if we ask anything according to his will, he hears us. And if we know that he hears us—whatever we ask—we know that we have what we asked of him"* (1 John 5:14, 15).

Expressing Your Faith Through Prayer

Prayer is one way of expressing your faith to God. If the prayer that follows expresses your sincere desire, consider praying the prayer or putting the thoughts into your own words:

Dear God, I need you. I acknowledge that I have been directing my own life and that, as a result, I have sinned against you. I thank you that you have forgiven my sins through Christ's death on the cross for me. I now invite Christ to take his place on the throne of my life. Take control of my life through the Holy Spirit as you promised you would if I asked in faith. I now thank you for directing my life and for empowering me through the Holy Spirit.

Walking in the Spirit

If you become aware of an area of your life (an attitude or an action) that is displeasing to God, simply confess your sin, and thank God that he has forgiven your sins on the basis of Christ's death on the cross. Accept God's love and forgiveness by faith, and continue to have fellowship with him.

If you find that you've taken back control of your life through sin—a definite act of disobedience—try this exercise, "Spiritual Breathing," as you give that control back to God.

1. Exhale. Confess your sin. Agree with God that you've sinned against him, and thank him for his forgiveness of it, according to 1 John 1:9 and Hebrews 10:1-25. Remember that confession involves repentance, a determination to change attitudes and actions.

2. Inhale. Surrender control of your life to Christ, inviting the Holy Spirit to once again take charge. Trust that he now directs and empowers you, according to the command of Galatians 5:16-17 and the promise of 1 John 5:14-15. Returning to your faith in God enables you to continue to experience God's love and forgiveness.

Revolutionizing Your Marriage

This new commitment of your life to God will enrich your marriage. Sharing with your spouse what you've committed to is a powerful step in solidifying this commitment. As you exhibit the Holy Spirit's work within you, your spouse may be drawn to make the same commitment you've made. If both of you have given control of your lives to the Holy Spirit, you'll be able to help each other remain true to God, and your marriage may be revolutionized. With God in charge of your lives, life becomes an amazing adventure.

Leader's Notes

Contents

About Leading a HomeBuilders Group **100**

About the Leader's Notes...**104**

Session One **105**

Session Two **108**

Session Three **111**

Session Four **113**

Session Five...**117**

Session Six **120**

About Leading a HomeBuilders Group

What is the leader's job?

Your role is that of "facilitator"—one who encourages people to think and to discover what Scripture says, who helps group members feel comfortable, and who keeps things moving forward.

What is the best setting and time schedule for this study?

This study is designed as a small group home Bible study. However, it can be adapted for use in a Sunday school setting as well. Here are some suggestions for using this study in a small group and in a Sunday school class:

In a small group

To create a friendly and comfortable atmosphere, it is recommended that you do this study in a home setting. In many cases the couple that leads the study also serves as host to the group. Sometimes involving another couple as host is a good idea. Choose the option you believe will work best for your group, taking into account factors such as the number of couples participating and the location.

Each session is designed as a ninety-minute study; but we recommend a two-hour block of time. This will allow you to move through each part of the study at a more relaxed pace. However, be sure to keep in mind one of the cardinal rules of a small group: Good groups start *and* end on time. People's time is valuable, and your group will appreciate you being respectful of this.

In a Sunday school class

There are two important adaptations you need to make if you want to use this study in a class setting: 1) The material you cover should focus on the content from the Blueprints section of each session. Blueprints is the heart of each session and is designed to last sixty minutes. 2) Most Sunday school classes are taught in a teacher format instead of a small group format. If this study will be used in a class setting, the class should adapt to a small group dynamic. This will involve an interactive, discussion-based format and may also require a class to break into multiple smaller groups (we recommend groups of six to eight people).

What is the best size group?

We recommend from four to eight couples (including you and your spouse). If you have more people interested than you think you can accommodate, consider asking someone else to lead a second group. If you have a large group, you are encouraged at various times in the study to break into smaller subgroups. This helps you cover the material in a timely fashion and allows for optimum interaction and participation within the group.

What about refreshments?

Many groups choose to serve refreshments, which help create an environment of fellowship. If you plan on including refreshments in your study, here are a couple of suggestions: 1) For the first session (or two) you should provide the refreshments and then allow the group to be involved by having people sign up to bring them on later dates. 2) Consider starting your group with a short time of informal fellowship and refreshments (fifteen minutes), then move into the study. If couples are late, they miss only the food and don't disrupt the study. You may also want to have refreshments available at the end of your meeting to encourage fellowship; but remember, respect the group members' time by ending the study on schedule and allowing anyone who needs to leave right away the opportunity to do so gracefully.

What about child care?

Groups handle this differently depending on their needs. Here are a couple of options you may want to consider:

- Have everyone be responsible for making their own arrangements.

- As a group, hire child care and have all the kids watched in one location.

What about prayer?

An important part of a small group is prayer. However, as the leader, you need to be sensitive to the level of comfort the people in your group have toward praying in front of others. Never call on people to pray aloud if you don't know if they are comfortable doing this. There are a number of creative approaches you can take, such as modeling prayer, calling for volunteers, and letting people state their prayers in the form of finishing a sentence. A tool that is helpful in a group is a prayer list. You are encouraged to do this, but let it be someone else's ministry to the group. You should lead the prayer time, but allow another couple in the group the opportunity to create, update, and distribute prayer lists.

In closing

An excellent resource that covers leading a HomeBuilders group in greater detail is the *HomeBuilders Leader Guide* by Drew and Kit Coons. This book may be obtained at your local Christian bookstore, or by contacting Group Publishing or FamilyLife.

About the Leader's Notes

The sessions in this study can be easily led without a lot of preparation time. However, accompanying Leader's Notes have been provided to assist you in preparation. The categories within the Leader's Notes are as follows:

Objectives

The purpose of the Objectives is to help focus the issues that will be presented in each session.

Notes and Tips

This section will relate any general comments about the session. This information should be viewed as ideas, helps, and suggestions. You may want to create a checklist of things you want to be sure to do in each session.

Commentary

Included in this section are notes that relate specifically to Blueprints questions. Not all Blueprints questions in each session will have accompanying commentary notes. Questions with related commentaries are designated by numbers (e.g. Blueprints question 8 in Session One would correspond to number 8 in the Commentary section of Session One Leader's Notes).

Session One:
Essentials for Establishing Growth as a Couple

Objectives

The Christian life is one of exciting growth as you establish a solid relationship with Christ.

In this session, couples will...

- discover that a Christian can grow in faith just as a person grows physically.
- examine what prevents some Christians from growing spiritually.
- learn essentials for spiritual growth.
- realize the importance of growing together spiritually as a couple.

Notes and Tips

1. If you have not already done so, you will want to read the information on pages 4 and 5 as well as "About Leading a HomeBuilders Group" and "About the Leader's Notes" starting on page 100.

2. As part of the first session, you may want to review with the group some Ground Rules (see page 12 in the Introduction).

3. Because this is the first session, make a special point to tell the group about the importance of the HomeBuilders Project. Encourage each couple to Make a Date for a time before the next meeting to complete the project. Mention that you will ask about this during the Warm-Up of the next session.

4. This is the first session, so you may want to offer a closing prayer instead of asking others to pray aloud. Many people are uncomfortable praying in front of others, and unless you already know your group well, it may be wise to slowly venture into various methods of prayer. Regardless of how you decide to close, you should serve as a model.

5. You may want to remind the group that because this group is just underway, it's not too late to invite another couple to join the group. Challenge everyone to think about couples they could invite to the next session.

6. In the Blueprints section for question 7, you may want to divide up the passage and look at one type of soil at a time.

Commentary

Here is some additional information about various Blueprints questions. The numbers that follow correspond to the Blueprints questions of the same numbers in the session. If you share any of these points, be sure to do so in a manner that does not stifle discussion by making you the authority with *the real answers*. Begin your comments by saying things like "One thing I notice in this passage is..." or "I think another reason for this is..."

2. The person described is someone who has not grown very much in his or her faith. This person is probably not spending much time reading the Bible and establishing a solid relationship with God. This person doesn't act much differently than a non-Christian.

4. A Christian needs proper nutrition to grow. This includes time in God's Word, fellowship with other Christians, communion with God through prayer and worship, and serving others.

5. Remaining in Jesus means seeking him, knowing him, and drawing upon his strength. As a branch, you are connected to Christ, and you draw your spiritual lifeblood from him.

7. One reason some Christians haven't grown much may be that they've never had someone close to them challenge them and model the Christian life for them.

10. It's kind of like climbing opposite sides of a triangle toward God at the top: As you get closer to God, you also get closer to each other.

Attention HomeBuilders Leaders

FamilyLife invites you to register your HomeBuilders group. Your registration connects you to the HomeBuilders Leadership Network, a worldwide movement of couples who are using HomeBuilders to strengthen marriages and families in their communities. You'll receive the latest news about HomeBuilders and other ministry opportunities to help strengthen marriages and families in your community. As the HomeBuilders Leadership Network grows, we will offer additional resources such as online training, prayer requests, and chat with authors. There is no cost or obligation to register; simply go to www.homebuildersgroup.com.

Session Two:

The Power of Prayer in Marriage

Objectives

Prayer promotes growth in your relationships with God and with your spouse.

In this session, couples will...

- recall what they learned about prayer as children.
- discover what the Bible says about the benefits of prayer.
- learn three components of prayer.
- understand how consistent prayer can improve their marriage relationship.

Notes and Tips

1. Since this is the second session, your group members have probably warmed up a bit to each other; however, they may not feel free to be completely open and honest about their marriage relationships. Don't force the issue, but continue encouraging couples to attend and to complete their projects.

2. You may wish to have extra study guides and Bibles for those who didn't bring theirs.

3. If someone joins the group for the first time this session, give a brief summary of the main points of Session One. Also, be sure to introduce those who do not know each other. You may want to have each new couple share their responses to the Warm-Up exercise in Session One.

4. Make sure the arrangements for refreshments (if you're planning to have them) are covered.

5. If your group has decided to use a prayer list, make sure this is covered.

6. If you told the group during the first session that you'd be asking them to share something they learned from the first HomeBuilders Project, be sure to ask them. This is an important time for you to establish an environment of accountability.

7. The section on the benefits of prayer is probably the most important section of this session. If your group members can understand that prayer doesn't have to be lifeless—that through prayer they can grow spiritually and experience God and experience his peace—they'll be motivated to pray more.

8. For the closing prayer in this session, you may want to ask for a volunteer or two to close the group in prayer. Check ahead of time with a couple of people you think might be comfortable praying aloud.

Commentary

2. Christian couples often know they should pray together, but just don't do it. They let other activities and priorities take precedence. They may

Note: The numbers here correspond to the Blueprints questions of the same numbers in the session.

also feel uncomfortable praying together as a couple.

3. Second Chronicles 7:14: Those who confess their sins and turn from their wicked ways will experience healing and forgiveness.
- Matthew 6:6: Experience God's reward.
- Matthew 26:41: Will not fall into temptation.
- Philippians 4:6-7: Receive God's peace.
- James 1:5: Receive wisdom.
- James 5:16: Experience healing.

5. Praising God means declaring who he is and what he has done for us. Worship and praise raise our awareness of God's presence in our lives. The more we praise God, the more we notice the ways he touches every aspect of our experience, and we begin to see our problems more in the context of God's power and control.

7. David wanted to restore his relationship with God. He was totally humble before God.

8. Confession restores our relationship with God after it has been damaged by sin.

9. Psalm 34:4-18 not only talks about what God will do to answer our prayers, but also what he does in our hearts when we pray.

10. God is eager for us to seek him, and we should approach God as a father who loves us deeply.

Session Three:

The Guidebook for Growth

Objectives

The greatest book ever written is God's gift to help you grow closer to him and to your spouse.

In this session, couples will…

- consider the value of the Bible as a resource for individuals and couples.

- recall experiences in which the Bible has provided specific benefits in their lives.

- practice using observation, interpretation, and application in the study of the Bible.

Notes and Tips

1. Congratulations. With the completion of this session, you will be halfway through this study. It's time for a checkup: How are you feeling? How is the group going? What has worked well so far? What things might you consider changing as you head into the second half?

2. Session Three features the Bible as not just the tool, but also as the topic. Called by some "the least read bestseller of all time," the Bible is often ignored by many of the same people who declare its benefits. As the leader, focus on showing group members that the Bible can change their lives! Use the Word with them. It's key that group members have a positive experience using the Word.

3. Remember the importance of starting and ending on time.

4. If you choose to do the "For Extra Impact" activity in the Wrap-Up, you'll need to have a puzzle—one that's too difficult to put together quickly without seeing the picture.

5. *Looking ahead:* For the Warm-Up in Session Four, you'll need an uninflated balloon for each person.

Commentary

Note: The numbers here correspond to the Blueprints questions of the same numbers in the session.

2. Today's culture accepts no standards for truth. For many, truth is subjective and depends on the situation, the person, and the need. But we know God's truth is truth for all time.

4. The Word of God helps us see the work of God in history. By remembering how God has worked in the past, we can get a glimpse of how he can work in our lives.

9. Too many people know what the Bible says, but don't act upon that knowledge. Without application you never use the principles and insights of the Word. Also, you will lose enthusiasm for further study if you aren't experiencing the joy of seeing God's Word make a difference in your lives.

Session Four:
Growing Together Through the Holy Spirit

Objectives

When you draw upon the Holy Spirit's power, you will experience growth in your life and in your marriage relationship.

In this session, couples will...

- recognize their need for God's help in living the Christian life.
- discuss Bible passages on what the Holy Spirit does within the life of the Christian.
- commit to living by the Holy Spirit.

Notes and Tips

1. For the Warm-Up activity in this session, you'll need an uninflated balloon for each person. Any size or shape will do.

2. The subject of this session is pivotal to the life of any Christian. It is the Holy Spirit who gives us the ability to live a life pleasing to God. Without the Spirit, we end up frustrated and defeated trying to live the Christian life in our own strength. For some in your group, recognizing the work of the Holy Spirit will provide brand-new spiritual insight and understanding. Others may know about the Holy Spirit's work, but need help to personally apply their knowledge. Still others may need to make a recommitment to live by the Spirit. Be in prayer before this session that all participants will be receptive to the Holy Spirit's gentle persuasion in their lives.

3. By this time group members should be getting more comfortable with each other. During the closing prayer, you may want to give everyone an opportunity to pray by asking the group to finish a sentence that goes something like this: "Lord, I want to thank you for…" Be sensitive to anyone who may not feel comfortable doing this.

4. For the Wrap-Up section: If people have trouble thinking of examples of the Holy Spirit working in their lives, share an example from your own life to get things started.

You might want to read aloud the explanation of how to give the Holy Spirit control of your life. Share how you have prayed similar prayers to allow God to control your life through the Holy Spirit. Then read the suggested prayer aloud and invite those who are prepared to live by the Holy Spirit to repeat it in their hearts. If you sense that people are struggling to give control of their lives to the Holy Spirit, encourage them to read "Our Problems, God's Answers" in the back of their books.

Commentary

Note: The numbers here correspond to the Blueprints questions of the same numbers in the session.

4. If you sense confusion in your group about who the Holy Spirit is, or if any group members are silent and don't know how to answer the question, use that as a springboard for the remainder of the session. Comment that this confusion and silence proves how real the problem is. Even Christians often don't understand who the Holy Spirit is.

John 14:16-17: Notice the prepositions used in these two verses: first, he will be "*with* you forever" (verse 16) and he "will be *in* you" (verse 17). These indicate that our relationship with the Holy Spirit is meant to be a very intimate one.

John 16:13-15: The Holy Spirit is our guide and helps us understand Scripture and discloses the will of God to us.

Acts 1:8: Notice that Jesus gives the command in the same breath that he mentions the power. He knows we cannot tell others about Christ without the power of the Holy Spirit.

Romans 8:26-27: The Holy spirit helps in prayer through interceding for us.

Second Timothy 1:14: The Holy Spirit dwells within us.

7. Living by the Spirit means a continual dependence upon the Holy Spirit for wisdom, guidance, and power.

8. The Holy Spirit will work in a heart that is humble toward God. Unconfessed sin can hinder the work of the Holy Spirit in us.

9. We should offer our bodies "as living sacrifices" to God. We should no longer conform ourselves to the world, but seek to fulfill God's will and live a life that is pleasing to him.

10. God will give us what we ask according to his will. Since we know his will for us is to be controlled by the Spirit, we know he will grant that request.

11. You can experience joy and peace from God.

Session Five:
Following Jesus

Objectives

Faithfully following Jesus will help you grow together in Christ and in your marriage.

In this session, couples will...

- examine the biblical explanation of the responsibilities, costs, and disciplines of discipleship.

- share experiences in which they have sought to live as Jesus' disciples.

- plan specific steps to take as a couple to love and serve others as Jesus' disciples.

Notes and Tips

1. This session and the next are the most challenging of the entire study. These final sessions will encourage your group members to commit their entire lives to following Christ.

2. Those in your group who have come to grips with the work of the Holy Spirit in their lives will welcome the practical help provided in this session. Those who still struggle with surrendering their will to that of the Spirit will also benefit from the insights this session brings about the implications of being a follower of Jesus. Those whose Christianity consists of casually aligning themselves with some of Jesus' teaching will be seriously challenged.

3. As leader, be sensitive to the varied levels of spiritual life among the members of your group. Lovingly nudge them all toward a life of more complete commitment. Openly share your own pilgrimage, letting people know of times you have struggled in following Jesus and the reasons why you continue seeking to be his disciple.

4. If you're willing to do the "For Extra Impact" activity in the Wrap-Up, you'll need to do considerable planning. You might want to think of some options in advance to talk about during this session.

5. As the leader of a small group, one of the best things you can do for your group is to pray specifically for each group member. Why not take some time to pray as you prepare for this session.

6. *Looking ahead:* If you're going to do the "For Extra Impact" activity in the Warm-Up section of Session Six, you'll need some modeling dough or clay for each person.

Commentary

Note: The numbers here correspond to the Blueprints questions of the same numbers in the session.

1. As Christians, Christ is our example, and we strive to live up to what he teaches us. However, if we are Christians, Christ is also at work in us. (See Romans 8:9-11 and Galatians 2:20.)

5. Following Jesus is not the same as being simply an armchair observer characterized by the statement: "I follow the Cubs; I check their place in the standings every week." Following

Jesus involves leaving other pursuits and committing ourselves to God's will for our lives no matter what he calls us
to do. It means making God the center of our lives.

11. Matthew 11:28-30: We will find rest for our souls.

Luke 18:28-30: Whatever we may have given up to follow
Christ will be given back to us many times over.

John 8:31-32: The truth of God's Word gives us great personal freedom.

John 10:9-10: In Christ there is abundant life.

Ephesians 3:20-21: God will do more in our lives than we
can imagine.

Session Six:
Making Disciples

Objectives

If you're growing together as a couple, you will reproduce yourselves spiritually and make an impact for God on generations to come.

In this session, couples will...

- explore biblical and personal evidence that God can use them to make disciples.

- discuss the need for Christian couples to share their faith through the power of the Holy Spirit.

- consider opportunities for becoming more effective in sharing their faith with others.

Notes and Tips

1. Christians are not meant to be just happy, contented people keeping the good news of Jesus Christ to themselves. Making disciples is both an outgrowth of and a catalyst for our growth in Christ. This session focuses on God's provision for us to supply the resources we need to reproduce ourselves spiritually. As the leader, you can help your group members learn to depend on the faithful presence of the Holy Spirit in their day-to-day opportunities for sharing Christ.

2. If you're going to do the "For Extra Impact" activity in the Warm-Up section, you'll need some modeling dough or clay for each person.

3. If you do the "For Extra Impact" activity in the Wrap-Up, you'll need a sheet of paper for each person.

4. While this HomeBuilders Couples Series has great value, people are likely to gradually return to previous patterns of living, unless they commit to a plan for carrying on the progress made. During this final session of the course, encourage couples to take specific steps beyond this series to keep their marriages growing. For example, you may want to challenge couples who have developed the habit of a "date night" during the course of this study to continue this practice. Also, you may want the group to consider doing another study from this series.

Commentary

1. Encourage people to think specifically about the analogy and how fishing relates to reaching others for Jesus. Here are a few thoughts: We need to go where the "fish" are, that is, where people needing Jesus live, work, and play. We also need to do those things that attract "fish." Fishers of men should look for ways to interest people in the gospel. For example, some non-Christians would be more likely to go with you to hear a well-known Christian football coach talk about his faith than to go with you to church.

Note: The numbers here correspond to the Blueprints questions of the same numbers in the session.

3. The most important thing we can offer to God is our willingness to serve him. God will use us if we let him.

4. Many are ready to come to Christ, but more Christians need to be willing to tell them how.

5. Taking a strong stand as a Christian may mean facing unfair criticism and ridicule.

6. God gives us the privilege of being used, but ultimately, God, through the work of the Holy Spirit, is responsible.

7. God wants all of us to tell others about him. We may each have contact with non-Christians who have little contact with any other Christians. You may want to have group members think of people they know in their neighborhoods or at work who God wants them to tell about Jesus.

8. To get people talking, you might want to tell about a situation where you had an opportunity to explain the gospel to someone. Focus on the indicators you noticed that made you feel the gospel should be shared.

Invite group members to share similar incidents from their experiences. If they find it difficult to think of appropriate situations, tell them to think of times they now recognize as potential opportunities, but may not have done so at the time.

11. If we have children, they will learn not only from our words, but from our personal example. They absorb our attitudes, our mannerisms, our weaknesses, and our strengths, whether we like it or not. And God has given us the responsibility to point them to him as they grow up.

Prayer Journal

Prayer Journal

Prayer Journal

Prayer Journal

Recommended Reading

Authentic Christianity, Ray Stedman

Balancing the Christian Life, Charles Ryrie

Discipleship, Billie Hanks and William Shell

The Green Letters, Miles J. Stanford

The Imitation of Christ, Thomas à Kempis

Improving Your Serve, Charles Swindoll

The Knowledge of the Holy, A.W. Tozer

Manners and Customs of the Bible, James M. Freeman

Master Plan of Evangelism, Robert Coleman

My Utmost for His Highest, Oswald Chambers

Power Through Prayer, E.M. Bounds

The Secret, Bill Bright

Too Busy Not to Pray, Bill Hybels

The Transferable Concept series, Bill Bright

What Christianity Is All About, Alan Scholes

What the Bible Is All About, Henrietta Mears

Witnessing Without Fear, Bill Bright

ACKNOWLEDGMENTS

The members of the PEACHTREE BOUQUET Committee wish to express their appreciation to the following members and friends of the Junior League of DeKalb County, Inc. who contributed recipes to this cookbook.

Patricia Henson Adams
Molly London Ahlquist
Laura Akin
Sandy Allen
Nancy Emery Anderson
Karen Modisteff Anderson
Susan McCeney Anderson
Betty Mitchell Anderson
Jeanine Craig Andrews
Joan Smith Ansley
Martha Armstrong
Deborah Dendy Ashendorf
Ellen Wogon Austin
Barrie Clark Aycock
Cheryl Williams Baxter
LoraLee Abbazia Beard
Beverly Hall Beaudrot
Libby Conner Beckham
Patty Shotton Begnaud
Melinda Sumner Belote
Virginia Shannon Binion
Sandy Southwell Bishop
Wendy Spatz Bishop
Anne Kabel Blount
Judith Alexander Bobo
Wanda Boylston
Marcia Taylor Brent
Tricia Hulsey Bridges
Barbara Brockman
Carolyn Bennett Broucek
Jane Black Buckler
Nancy Parham Buckler
Catherine Chalk Builder
Nancy Stevens Burriss
Carol Preller Bush
Kathy Hastings Cable
Lynn Callahan Goodroe
Joye Baldwin Callaway
Betty Jeanne Ellison Candler
Karna Thomas Candler
Judy Rutland Carlsen
Victoria Willis Carpenter
Barbara Carson
Christina Carson
Virginia McSwain Carson
Katherine Triplitt Carter
Marge Davis Carter

Lyn Kilgo Cates
Mary Cawthon
Elaine Suess Chambers
Nancy Hooks Chambers
Missy Arnold Chapman
Julie Childs
Jeanne Chimelewski
Penn Weitnauer Clark
Jo Ann Fox Clark
Cissy Smith Cleveland
Charon Hodgens Clymer
Pam Thomas Colbenson
Jeannie Moore Conner
Janet McKnight Cook
Nancy Waring Corbitt
Caroline Moore Cribbs
Shelley Cross
Kate Livingston Cucchi
Joy Ballew Culbreth
Donna Fort Davidson
Nancy Palmer DeBaun
Sally Gay Dickey
Lynn Diversi
Whitney Dodd
Marlene Odom Duke
Cheryl Cooper Dunbar
Jeannie Nettles Dyson
Jane Fackler Edmonds
Deborah Patterson Edmonston
Beth McDaniel Edwards
Jan McCorkle Espy
Barbara Chandler Evans
Jennifer Slocumb Ewing
Becky Anderson Fern
Jan Fleischman
Liz Copelan Ford
Gayle Parks Forehand
Toni Fowler
Susan Fox
Elaine Byars Franklin
Donna Bastian Fullilove
Claire Perdue Furth
Janet Dorsett Gallagher
Meg Gates
June Gay
Eugenia Johnson Giles
Katherine Schob Glenn

Joanne West Goldman
Linda Vaughn Goldsmith
Susan Horton Gray
Rita Green
Shirley Markuson Guhl
Patricia Rives Haase
Marty Halyburton
Michele Hanft
Motsy Gregory Hanna
Jan Journey Harben
Betsy Aitken Harrell
Mary Ezell Harrington
Jane Fleming Harris
Jill Cofer Harris
Lynda Gardner Harris
Ellen Cottraux Head
Louise Hebbeler
Vivki Keck Hedrick
Laura Whelchel Henderson
Linda Dennon Herren
Nancy James Hilley
Cary Boyd Hobbs
Diane Bell Hobbs
Doug Holder
Joanne Kennamer Hood
Donna Hooker
Susan Snow Hope
Lynn Ely Hornsby
Sally Evans Hovis
Jane McMullan Howe
Darlene Huggins
Pam Parsons Hughes
Linda Campbell Hull
Pam Foell Hunt
Valerie Hunt
Becky Ericsson Hunter
Marianne Hunter
Laura Tomlinson Jackson
Lyn Young Jackson
Edna Kronebitter Jennings
Sandy Floyd Jernigan
Allison Thomas Johnson
Ginny Waters Johnston
Cindy Tolleson Jollay
Kathryn Tolleson Jollay
Mimi Thomas Kee
Paulette Childers Keith
Angel Diogo Keller
Chris Liles Kendrick
Lynn Cunningham Kessler
Nancy Bass Kirby
Julie Edwards Kitchen
Linda Holley Kjorlaug
Kathy Gunville Kline

Beryl Kramer
Mary Ellen Kubis
Cecilia Henry Kurland
Ellen Lappa
Carolyn Gatling Lassiter
Marianne Boylston Lassiter
Maggie Douglas Lawson
Nancy Whitten Leathers
Sandy Smith Lee
Becky Lewis Lester
Jill Hastings Letts
Alice Liles
Donna Raynor Livingston
Lynne Pickens Lock
Nancy Burns Luckey
Nancy Layton Lundstrom
Sally Daniel Maloof
Elizabeth Marsh
Mary McKee Martin
Joan Wynne Mathews
Anne McCoun
Barbara Smith McCoy
Ann Tee McCrory
Susan Rutland McCullar
Genet McIntosh
Sally Moffett McKenna
Betsi Britten McLure
Libby McMahan
Altine McQueen
Kathleen McWalters
Margaret McWalters
Rae Dennir McWhirter
Leslie Hughes Meiere
May Michalko
Carol Spruill Miller
Marty Kelley Mitchell
Flip Sthreshley Moehlman
Linda Gregory Moffett
Sally Morris
Susan Myers
Judith Ann Stish Nathan
Denise Fast Neely
Peggy New
Becky Reynolds Nicholson
Marsha Stevens O'Connor
Gay O'Neal
Johnnie Milam Oliver
Susan Dangler Ozburn
Lisa Pardue
Lissy Makay Parker
Ginny Williams Parks
Margaret Partridge
Sallie Garrison Paschal

Kathy Patterson
Sara Munch Paulk
Sally Jenkins Peavy
Nancy Reese Pecora
Corrine Peek
Mallory Divine Perdue
Dottie Lowery Phillips
Kimberly Bacon Pickens
Patricia Vandiver Powell
Karla Chamness Preston
Cindy Gregory Raines
Verna Mobley Rauschenberg
Nancy Meyers Ray
Nikki Kneale Reifeis
Dianne Ramey Reynolds
Robin Rhodes
Marsha Allen Richardson
Angie Nations Richardson
Betsy Painter Roberts
Carol Newsome Roberts
Susan Paul Roche
Nancy Levering Rozzelle
Hazel Risley Rutland
Lynn Sarpy
Evon Scales
Irene Scales
Margaret McWalters Scales
Ginn Spears Schmeelk
Nancy Kelly Schoeler
Barbara Rick Schuyler
Fran Lamby Scott
Lacey Scruggs
Carolyn Seidel
Cara Shaw
John Shaw
Sally McArthur Shigley
Mary Alice Shinall
Karen Vaughn Shinall
Lois Deutschberger Shingler
Marylee Glover Sleeth

Pat O'Callaghan Smith
Sallie Biggs Smith
Linda Mozley Smith
Ellen Phillips Smith
Dottie Haisten Spencer
Vicky Spruill
Vicki Kudlacz Stafford
Mary Leith Stanfield
Kay Wilson Stewart
Frances Carringer Stinson
Lisa Kirk Stovall
Bobbi Stuart
Anne Diveley Sumpter
Sally Beggs Thomas
Carolyn Thompson
Jane Huie Thrash
Claire Johnson Tolleson
Kathy Gillespie Tomajko
Kathy Spence Tribble
Pattie Jackson Tuggle
Hilde Beskin Van Houten
Gail Potter Vrana
June Lanier Wagner
Joanne Guardiani Warlick
Rita Warren
Ellen Warthen
Ginny Kellum Watt
Mary Jo Graham Wells
Linda Simpson Wells
Susan Harris West
Janis Whitehead
Ellen McHalffey Widener
Jeanne Keokenberg Williams
Barbara Scanlon Williams
Judy Kapp Winder
Deborah Long Wingate
Anne Workman
Kathy Mueller Wright
Judy Yates
Mary Carson Young

We want to express our special appreciation to Allen Lindley with Happy Herman's and Verney E. Bentley, III for their assistance in suggesting wines to complement the entrees.

387

The members of the PEACHTREE BOUQUET Committee also wish to express their appreciation to the following Special Contributors who submitted recipes that helped to make this a unique and outstanding cookbook.

Hank Aaron
The Abbey Restaurant
Affairs to Remember Caterers
Anthonys Restaurant
The Atlanta Athletic Club-
    Executive Chef Ray Farmer
Jean Benton, Benton and
    Associates, Inc. Caterers
Bone's Steak and Seafood
    restaurant
Bosco's Ristorante Italiano
Olive Ann Burns
Skip Caray
G. Clisby Clarke
Bill Curry
Barbara and Vince Dooley
Nathalie Dupree
East 48th Street Market
The Georgian Club - Chef Mohammad
    Bakhtiari
Joyce Gould, Caterer
Elise Griffin, Peasant
    Restaurants, Inc.
Bob Harrell, Bob's Barbeque
Hedgerose Heights Inn

Herren's restaurant
Houlihan's Restaurant
McKinnon's Louisiane Restaurant
The Mansion restaurant
Manuel's Tavern - Bessie
    Johnson
Marra's Seafood Grill
R. L. Mathis Dairy
Lt. Governor Zell Miller
Wayland Moore
Mortons of Chicago
Pano's and Paul's Restaurant
Pearl's Fish Cafe
Peasant Uptown restaurant
Pittypat's Porch
Proof of the Pudding Caterers
Homer Rice
Willard Scott
Kathy Grizzard Smook
Mrs. Pat Swindall
Trotters Restaurant
Ted Turner
Jeff Van Note
The Wright Gourmet Shoppe

-A-
ALMOND
  and Mandarin Orange
    Salad, 357
  and Mushrooms with Wild
    Rice, 131
  Biscuit Tortoni, 341
  Curried Fruit, 290
  Honey Dressing, 92
  Orange Chicken, 217
  Peach-Glazed Cake, 303
  Red Snapper Almondine,
    161
  Roca, 379
  Torte, 313
AMARETTO
  Chocolate Bars, 333
  Freeze, 32
  Mousse, 338
  Pie, 314
  Sauce, 353
Amberjack, Grilled, 141
Angel Strawberry Cake, 309
Antipasto, Holiday, 12
APPETIZERS
  Cold
    Candied Citrus Pecans,
      16
    Caviar Pie, 9
    Cheese Straws, 17
    Cream Cheese and
      Bacon Tea Sandwiches,
      10
    Elegant and Easy Brie, 28
    Garlic Olives, 24
    Glazed Bacon with
      Walnuts, 11
    Glazed Nuts, 15
    Hidden Treasure, 26
    Holiday Antipasto, 12
    Marinated Vegetables, 31
    Pickled Shrimp, 29
    Salmon Rolls, 28
    Shrimp Pizza, 30
  Dips
    Almond-Honey Dressing,
      92
    Cheesy Dip Surprise, 15
    Chili Relleno, 23
    Clam, 19
    Divine, 22
    Ground Beef, 23
    Honey, 221
    Honey-Mustard
      Dressing, 93
    Hot and Sweet
      Mustard, 230
    Hot Nacho, 22
    Miss Daisey's Crabmeat,
      20
    Onion Rye, 21
    Rebecca Sauce, 27
    Snappy Vegetable, 358
    Tarama Salata, 31

  Hot
    Appetizer Gougère, 13
    Blend of the Bayou
      Seafood Casserole, 253
    Bone's Beer-Battered
      Shrimp, 153
    Crab Grass, 20
    Cranberry Meatballs, 9
    Easy Fried Cheese, 11
    Egg Rolls, 24
    Far East Shrimp Balls, 30
    Garlic Shrimp in Lemon-
      Wine Sauce, 359
    Hawaiian Chicken
      Wings, 17
    Hot Crabmeat Canapés,
      19
    Italian Cheese Rolls, 14
    Mandarin Ham Rolls,
      185
    Mushroom Squares, 25
    Parmesan Onion
      Canapés, 21
    Pearls' Fried Crabmeat
      Puffs, 144
    Phyllo Pastries, 18
    Sausage Party Pizzas, 26
    Sausage Pinwheels, 22
    Sesame Chicken with
      Honey Dip, 220
    Shrimp Manallé, 156
    Swiss Cheese Soufflé,
      133
  Spreads and Molds
    Asparagus-Lobster
      Cocktail Mousse, 10
    Bacon Ball, 11
    Ceviche, 358
    Delicious Liver Pâté, 25
    Garlic Cheese Ball, 16
    Holiday Cheese Ball, 13
    Hot Crab Spread, 20
    Olive and Cream Cheese
      Ball, 14
    Oyster Log, 28
    Salmon Mousse, 27
    Shrimp Mousse, 29
    Spicy Cheese Ball, 14
    Strawberry Cheese Ball,
      16
    Tuna Spread, 360
APPLE(S)
  and Cornflakes, My
    Mother's, 289
  Caramel Fondue, 354
  Favorite Chops in
    Casserole, 250
  Molded Waldorf Salad, 89
  Noodle Pudding with Fruit,
    339
  Orange-Anise Spice Bags,
    38
  Pecan Upside-Down Pie,
    316

  Red Candy, 339
  Spiced Bourbon Punch,
    32
  Stuffed, 88
APRICOT(S)
  and Prune Coffeecake,
    116
  Hot Casserole, 290
  Wafer Dessert, 341
ARTICHOKE(S)
  and Chicken Rice Salad,
    63
  and Ham Casserole, 248
  and Ripe Olive Salad, 76
  and Tuna, 256
  Chicken Casserole, 215
  Poulet De Susie, 228
  Salmon in Foil, 148
  Scalloped, 267
  Soup, 51
  with Shrimp, 252
ASPARAGUS
  Beef Salad with Broccoli
    and, 64
  Casserole, 259
  Fettuccini with, 124
  Lobster Cocktail Mousse,
    10
  Marinated, 267
  Mornay, 268
  Spring Vegetable Sauté
    276
AVOCADO
  Avocado Soup, Chilled
    Creamy, 60
  Avocado Crab, 142
  Green and Gold Salad, 72
-B-
BACON
  Ball, 11
  Cream Cheese Tea
    Sandwiches, 10
  Glazed with Walnuts, 11
Baked Chicken Breasts, 201
Baked Chicken, Tangy, 214
Baked Chicken, Soy, 227
Baked Fish, Delicious, 160
Baked Ham Mornay, 249
Baked Rice, 262
Baked Stuffed Pumpkin, 291
Baked Stuffed Snapper, 162
Baked Swiss Chicken, 201
BANANA(S)
  Doris' Punch, 33
  Pineapple-Nut Cake, 301
  Split Cake, 296
BARBECUE
  Bar-B-Que Spareribs and
    Meatballs, 192
  Beef Stuffed Pork Roast,
    193
  Chicken, Commander
    Burn's, 208
  Mimi's Bar-B-Que, 191

Barbecued Lima Beans, 278
Barley Pilaf, 368
Basic Steps to Making Bread, 97
Bavarian Cream, Rosebud's, 342
BEAN(S)
　Green Beans (See Separate Listing)
　Hearty Sausage Soup, 43
　Hot Dish, 259
BEEF
　Beer Steak Stroganoff, 180
　Bourguignon, 237
　Brunswick Stew, 168
　Chicken Kabobs, 171
　Chipped Casserole, 238
　Corned and Cabbage, Irish Style, 183
　Dijon, 369
　Flank Steak with Fresh Basil-Tomato Sauce, 176
　Ginger Grilled London Broil, 177
　Manuel's Greek Salad, 72
　Marinade for London Broil, 177
　Marinated Roast Sandwiches, 178
　Munich "Sauerbraten", 179
　Oriental Flank Steak with Rice, 174
　Ragout, 240
　Roast for Sandwiches, 178
　Roast Tenderloin, 182
　Salad with Broccoli and Asparagus, 64
　Scotched Filet Mignon with Fresh Mushroom Sauce, 174
　Steak in a Bag, 180
　Steak Tournedos, 175
　Stuffed Pork Roast, 193
　Sukiyaki, 173
　Whiskey-Glazed Corned, 184
BEEF, GROUND
　Baked Rotelle with, 125
　Bar-B-Que Spareribs and Meatballs, 192
　Bob's Brunswick Stew, 167
　Cabbage Casserole, 240
　Chili Seasoning, 198
　Cranberry Meatballs, 9
　Dip, 23
　Hot Nacho Dip, 22
　Enchilada Cheese Towers, 170
　Mexican Salad, 66
　Noodle Bake, 239
　One Meal Dish, 241
　Oriental Spaghetti, 238

Picadillo, 181
Po Boy Fillets, 172
Polynesian Goulash, 239
Salami, 172
Vegetable Medley Soup, 59
Zucchini Bake, 242
Beer Batter, 144
Beer Beef Steak Stroganoff, 180
BEVERAGES
　Amaretto Freeze, 32
　French Hot Chocolate, 34
　Ginger's Egg Nog, 36
　Hot Buttered Rum Mix, 32
　Hot Mocha Mix, 35
　Hot Spiced Wine, 40
　It's Almost Bailey's, 40
　Kahlua Velvet Frosty, 36
　Microwave Cappuccino, 34
　Orange-Anise Spice Bags, 38
　Punch
　　Champagne, 35
　　Doris' Banana, 33
　　Pineapple-Champagne, 34
　　Spiced Bourbon-Apple, 32
　　Tequila-Champagne, 38
　　Sherry Sour, 39
　　Sneaky Petes, 37
　　Tea
　　　Decaffinated Spiced Mix, 33
　　　Hot Florida, 39
　　　Long Island Iced, 39
　　　Perculator Hot Fruit, 37
　　　Spiced Iced, 38
　　　White Sangria, 36
Bird Feeder Candles, 384
BISCUITS
　Biscuits, 223
　Cheese, 111
　Quick, 111
　Tortoni, 341
Black Bottom Pie, 315
Blue Cheese Soufflé, 133
Braised Pork Tenderloin, 190
BRAN
　Muffins, 362
　Pineapple Muffins, 109
　Six Week Muffins, 110
Brandied Poached Pears, 375
Brazilian Rice, 129
BREADS
　Basic Steps to Making, 97
　Biscuits (See Separate Listing)
　Cheese Bread Sticks, 100
　Cheese Blintzes, 134
　Coffeecake and Sweet Breads

Apricot and Prune, 116
　Bishop's, 107
　Pluck It Cake, 112
　Sweet Rolls From Herren's, 115
　Corn Sticks, 110
　Dandy-Quicky Doughnuts, 102
　Dumplings and Chicken, 218
　Fabulous French Toast, 117
　Five Minute Microwave Croutons, 117
　Herb Butter, 118
　Homemade Croutons, 50
　Muffins (See Separate Listing)
　Patriotic Pastries, 380
　Quick
　　Cheese French, 99
　　Chocolate Zucchini, 100
　　Cranberry Orange Tea, 101
　　Ham and Cheese, 101
　　Herb Tomato, 103
　　Irish Raisin, 104
　　Poppy Seed, 105
　　Strawberry, 106
　Rolls (See Separate Listing)
　Soft Pretzels, 118
　Yeast
　　Brown, 99
　　Cheese Sticks, 100
　　Herb Cheese, 98
　　Proscuitto and Onion, 106
　　Spinach, 104
　　The Market's Crusty, 102
　　White Batter, 103
BROCCOLI
　Cheese Soup Supreme, 44
　Chowder, 45
　Company Ham Casserole, 250
　Fresh Vegetable Marinade, 83
　Mold, 74
　Oriental Sesame Chicken Dinner, 226
　Puff, 271
　Special, 271
　Stuffed Tomatoes, 269
　Stuffed Vidalia Onions, 270
　Swiss Chicken, 219
　Tree Top Marinade, 82
Broiled Zucchini, 367
BROWNIE(S)
　Chocolate Amaretto Bars, 333
　Coffee Torte, 311
　Crème De Menthe, 332

German Cheesecake, 331
Marshmallow-Fudge, 330
BRUNCH
Cheese Blintzes, 134
Cheese Strata, 136
Creole Eggs, 122
Easy Swiss Cheese Pie, 138
Eggs, 121
Fancy Egg Scramble, 123
Herb Cheese Grits, 132
Irresistible Spinach Quiche, 135
Puff, 134
Shrimp Eggs, 122
Willard Scott's Cheese Grits Soufflé, 132
Brunswick Stew, 168
Brunswick Stew, Bob's, 167
Brussels, Sprouts, Deviled, 269
Butter, Herb, 118
Butter Rolls, 114
Butterflied Leg of Lamb, 189
Buttermilk-Garlic Dressing, 93
Butterscotch Cookies, Filled, 326
-C-
CABBAGE
and Corned Beef, Irish Style, 183
Beef Casserole, 240
Sweet and Sour Soup, 44
CAJUN
Crawfish Monica, 146
Hoppinjohn Jambalaya, 196
Maque Choux, 260
CAKE
Amalgamation, 295
Angel Strawberry, 309
Banana Split, 296
Cheesecake (See Separate Listing)
Chess, 304
Chocolate-Cinnamon, 305
Chocolate Truffle, 304
Cocoa-Nut Layer, 302
Colonial Strawberry, 308
Flower Potcakes, 300
1/2 Pound, 296
Lane, 306
Peach-Glazed Almond, 303
Pineapple-Banana Nut, 301
Pumpkin Squares, 334
Walnut Yule Log, 310
White Chocolate, 312
Wonderful Spice, 307
CANDY
Almond Roca, 379
Caramel Corn Jacks, 382

Chocolate Truffles, 337
Colored Popcorn Balls, 352
English Toffee, 336
Haystacks, 295
Lollipops, 308
Peanut Logs, 336
Peanut Play Dough, 380
Pecan Pralines, 337
Popcorn Balls, 382
Cappuccino Cheesecake, 299
CARAMEL
Apple Fondue, 354
Baked Pears with, 351
Corn Jacks, 382
CARROTS
Lyonnaise, 272
Mold, 273
Scalloped, 273
Spring Vegetable Sauté, 276
Cashew Chicken, 244
Cashews, Glazed, 15
CASSEROLE(S)
Cheesy Spinach, 285
Chicken Artichoke, 215
Chicken Lasagna for a Crowd, 243
Fruit
Almond Curried Fruit, 290
Cranberry Conserve, 264
Hot Apricot Casserole, 290
Party Pineapple, 291
Meat/Main Dish
Baked Ham Mornay, 249
Beef Bourguignon, 237
Beef Ragout, 240
Blend of the Bayou Seafood, 253
Cabbage Beef, 240
Cashew Chicken, 244
Cheesy Egg Bake, 248
Chicago-Style Crab, 142
Chicken Chow Mein, 370
Chicken Delight, 244
Chicken Provencale, 250
Chicken Rice Elegante, 246
Chili Relleno, 247
Chipped Beef, 238
Company Ham, 250
Company Seafood Dinner, 254
Do-Ahead Seafood Bake, 254
Enchilada Cheese Towers, 170
Favorite Chops in Casserole, 250
Ground Beef Noodle

Bake, 239
Ham and Artichoke, 248
Hot Chicken Salad, 242
Lasagnette, 169
One Dish Meal, 241
Oriental Spaghetti, 238
Oysters Rockefeller, 146
Polynesian Goulash, 239
Poulet Au Frommage, 246
Sausage Rice, 252
Sauté De Veau Marengo, 258
Scalloped Oysters, 148
Seafood, 255
Seafood Supreme, 152
Shrimp A La Grecque, 157
Shrimp and Crab Rice, 256
Shrimp with Artichokes, 252
Sweet and Sour Lamb, 251
Tuna and Artichokes, 256
Veal Stroganoff, 257
Zucchini-Ground Beef Bake, 242
Vegetable
Asparagus, 259
Baked Rice, 262
Cajun Maque Choux, 260
Cheesy Potato Casserole, 283
Corn and Zucchini, 275
Creamed Onions and Peas, 281
Eggplant-Tomato Bake, 278
Golden Eggplant, 260
Green Bean, 261
Hot Bean Dish, 259
Okra Tomato Bake, 280
Onion, 261
Overnight Potatoes, 284
Scalloped Potatoes Au Gratin, 262
Special Broccoli, 271
Squash, 263
Tomato Cheese, 263
CAULIFLOWER
Curried Baked, 272
Fresh Vegetable Marinade, 83
Tree Top Marinade, 82
Caviar Pie, 9
CELEBRITY
Barbara Dooley,s Stir-Fried Shrimp with Fried Rice, 159
Brunswick Stew, 168
Chicken Carolina, 225
Chocolate Rum Pie, 317

Company Ham Casserole, 250
"Hunker Down" Foolproof Hollandaise Sauce, 292
Mexican Salad, 66
New Orleans Oyster Sandwich, 147
Porky's Revenge, 194
Quick Mud Pie, 320
Rosebud's Bavarian Cream, 342
Sweet Potato Soufflé, 288
Swiss Chicken, 219
Tomato Cheese Casserole, 263
Turnip Green and Cream Soup, 58
Willard Scott's Cheese Grits Soufflé, 132
Ceviche, 358
Chalupas, 196
Champagne Pineapple Punch, 34
Champagne Punch, 35
CHEESE
  and Ham Bread, 101
  and Macaroni, Deluxe, 136
  and Macaroni, Low-Cal, 373
  and Macaroni Salad, 78
  and Macaroni with Wine, 135
  and Tomato Salad, 363
  Appetizer Gougère, 13
  Bacon Ball, 11
  Biscuits, 111
  Blintzes, 134
  Bread Sticks, 100
  Broccoli Soup Supreme, 44
  Cheesy Egg Bake, 248
  Chicken Noodle Soup, 47
  Chowder, 57
  Cream Cheese and Bacon Tea Sandwiches, 10
  Dip Surprise, 15
  Easy Fried, 11
  Elegant and Easy Brie, 28
  Enchilada Cheese Towers, 170
  French Bread, 99
  Garlic Ball, 16
  Herb Bread, 98
  Herb Grits, 132
  Holiday Ball, 13
  Italian Rolls, 14
  Microwave Potato Soup, 54
  Olive and Cream Cheese Ball, 14
  Parmesan Onion Canapés, 21
  Queso, 138
  Spicy Ball, 14

Spinach Pasta with Mushroom Sauce, 372
Spinach Squares, 285
Strata, 136
Strawberry Ball, 16
Straws, 17
Tomato Casserole, 263
Willard Scott's Grits Soufflé, 132
CHEESECAKE
  Black Forest, 298
  Chocolate Velvet, 297
  Cappuccino, 299
  Cara's, 298
  Chestnut, 300
  German Brownie, 331
Cheesy Potato Casserole, 283
Cheesy Spinach Casserole, 285
Cheesy Squash Dressing, 286
Cherry Squares, 335
Chess Cake, 304
Chess Pie, Classic, 317
Chess Pie, Pineapple, 318
Chestnut Cheesecake, 300
CHICKEN
  and Artichoke Rice Salad, 63
  and Dumplings, 218
  and Peanuts in Hot Sauce, 224
  and Vegetable Sauté, 371
  Artichoke Casserole, 215
  Baked Breasts, 201
  Baked Swiss, 201
  Beef Kabobs, 171
  Bessie's, 202
  Bob's Brunswick Stew, 167
  Breast of Florentine, 222
  Breasts in Currant Jelly Sauce, 216
  Carolina, 225
  Cashew, 244
  Casserole Delight, 244
  Chaufroid, 221
  Cheesy Noodle Soup, 47
  Chow Mein, 370
  Chunky Corn Chowder, 48
  Commander Burns' Barbecue, 208
  Crescent Squares, 184
  Curried and Eggplant Stew, 224
  Curried Salad, 370
  Curry Mousse, 207
  Deviled, 202
  Enchilada Soup, 50
  Florentine, 226
  Fried with Cream Gravy, 203
  Gumbo, 48

Hawaiian Wings, 17
Hot Salad Casserole, 242
In Champagne Sauce, 204
Lasagna for a Crowd, 243
Lemon, 205
Main Dish Rice Salad, 66
Maple-Pecan, 208
Moravian, 209
Nuggets, 204
Orange Almond, 217
Oriental Salad, 63
Oriental Sesame Dinner, 226
Pecan-Breaded, 216
Phyllo Pastries, 18
Poppy Seed, 211
Poulet Au Frommage, 246
Poulet De Susie, 228
Provencale, 245
Rice Elegante, 246
Roast Stuffed with Orzo, 213
Scallopini, 220
Sesame Chicken with Honey Dip, 220
Sherried Parmesan, 211
Sopa De Pollo Y Maiz, 46
Southern Pie, 223
Soy Baked, 227
Stuffed Breasts with Dill Butter Sauce, 206
Stuffed Teriyaki, 229
Sukh, 228
Swiss, 219
Tangy Baked, 214
Tarragon Salad, 364
Tarragon with Angel Hair Pasta, 214
Waterzooi, 49
Wild Rice Salad, 64
with Mushroom-Wine Sauce, 210
with Sherried Cheese Sauce, 212
Chiffy Chaffy, 287
Chili Seasoning, 198
Chili Relleno Casserole, 247
Chive Sauce, Neta's, 292
CHOCOLATE
  Almond Roca, 379
  Baker's Pie, 314
  Black Bottom Pie, 315
  Black Forest Cheesecake, 298
  Bonbons, 335
  Brownies (See Separate Listing)
  Charlotte Au, 344
  Cinnamon Cake, 305
  Cocoa-Nut Layer Cake, 302
  Coffee Brownie Torte, 311
  Crepes, 345
  Crispy Chip Cookies, 329

Flower Potcakes, 300
French Hot, 34
Frozen Parfait, 347
Ice Cream Roll, 346
Kiss Cookies, 329
Marquis, 348
Meringues, 334
Nutty Buddy, 348
Pinwheel Cookies, 328
Rum Pie, 317
Silk, 374
Snowball, 349
Stuffed Apples, 88
Truffle Cake, 304
Truffles, 337
Velvet Cheesecake, 297
Walnut Yule Log, 310
White Cake, 312
Wows, 327
Zucchini Bread, 100
CHOWDER
   Broccoli, 45
   Cheese, 57
   Chunky Corn, 48
   Iowa Corn, 47
Chutney, Plum, 268
Cinnamon Chocolate Cake,
   305
Cinnamon Sweet Rolls From
   Herren's, 115
Clam Dip, 19
Clam Sauce with Pasta, 126
Clay, Modeling, 383
Coconut Cream Pie, 318
COFFEE
   Brownie Torte, 311
   It's Almost Bailey's, 40
   Kahlua Supreme, 350
   Microwave Cappuccino,
   34
Coffeecake (See Breads)
COOKIES
   Brownies (See Separate
   Listing)
   Candy Cane Cookies, 342
   Cherry Squares, 335
   Chocolate Bonbons, 335
   Chocolate Kiss, 329
   Chocolate Meringues, 334
   Chocolate Pinwheel, 328
   Chocolate Wows, 327
   Christmas Tree Cones, 312
   Crispy Chip, 329
   Filled Butterscotch, 326
   Gingerbread Men, 324
   Great-Grandmother's Tea,
   328
   Honey Puffs, 327
   Melting Moments, 332
   Orange Date-Nut Bars, 331
   Saltine Treats, 380
CORN
   and Zucchini, 275
   Cajun Maque Choux, 260
   Chunky Chowder, 48

Corn Sticks, 110
Frogmore Stew, 155
Grandma's Pudding, 275
Iowa Chowder, 47
Salad, 71
Savory Baked Pie, 274
Sopa De Pollo Y Maiz, 46
Corned Beef and Cabbage,
   Irish Style, 183
Corned Beef, Whiskey-
   Glazed, 184
Cornish Hens, Roast with
   Wild Rice Stuffing, 233
Cornish Hens with Apricot
   Glaze, 230
CRAB(MEAT)
   and Shrimp Rice
   Casserole, 256
   Avocado, 142
   Chicago-Style, 142
   Grass, 20
   Hot Canapés, 19
   Hot Spread, 20
   Miss Daisey's Dip, 20
   Pasta Seafood Salad, 69
   Pearl's Fried Puffs, 144
   Seafood Soup, 56
   Stuffed Fish Fillets, 149
   Trotters' Linguini with, 143
CRANBERRY(IES)
   Congealed Surprise, 84
   Conserve, 264
   Frozen Dream Salad, 83
   Holiday Cranberry Mold,
   84
   Meatballs, 9
   Orange Tea Bread, 101
Crawfish Monica, 146
Crawfish Soufflé, 145
Creole, Shrimp, 154
Creole Eggs, 122
Crème De Menthe Brownies,
   332
Crepes, Chocolate
   Chocolate, 345
CROUTONS
   Butter Toasted, 77
   Five Minute Microwave,
   117
   Homemade, 50
CUCUMBER
   Cold Soup, 54
   Cold Soup with Dill, 361
   Creamy Spinach Soup, 55
   Crisp Pickles, 68
Curried, Baked
   Cauliflower, 272
Curried, Chicken and
   Eggplant Stew, 224
Curried Chicken Salad,
   370
Curried Fish Soup, 360
Curried Fruit, Almond,
   290

Curried Seafood Salad,
   160
Curry Dressing, 73
Curry Mousse, Chicken,
   207
Curry Rice Mix, Fruited,
   130
CUSTARD
   Pie, Easy, 319
   Vanilla Cream, 347
   White Wine, 376
-D-
Date Orange Nut Bars, 331
DESSERTS
   Almond-Honey Dressing,
   92
   Amaretto Mousse, 338
   Apricot Wafer, 341
   Baked Pears with Caramel,
   351
   Biscuit Tortoni, 341
   Brandied Poached Pears,
   375
   Cakes (See Separate
   Listing)
   Candies (See Separate
   Listing)
   Caramel Apple Fondue,
   354
   Cardinal Strawberries, 352
   Charlotte Au Chocolate,
   344
   Chocolate Chocolate
   Crepes, 345
   Chocolate Ice Cream Roll,
   346
   Chocolate Marquis, 348
   Chocolate Snowball, 349
   Cookies (See Separate
   Listing)
   Fancy Fruit Kabobs, 352
   Fresh Strawberries in
   Grand Marnier Sauce,
   353
   Frostings and Fillings (See
   Separate Listing)
   Frozen Chocolate Parfait,
   347
   Frozen Lemon Delight,
   350
   Kahlua Supreme, 350
   Nutty Buddy, 348
   Pies (See Separate Listing)
   Pineapple Cream Delight,
   351
   Pudding (See Separate
   Listing)
   Rosebud's Bavarian
   Cream, 342
   Sauces and Toppings (See
   Separate Listing)
   Strawberry Bavarian
   Cream, 344
   Strawberry Surprise, 366
   Tortes (See Separate

Listing)
Vanilla Cream Custard, 347
White Wine Custard, 376
Deviled Brussels Sprouts, 269
Deviled Chicken, 202
Dips (See Appetizers)
Doughnuts, Dandy-Quicky, 102
Doves, Smothered, 231
Doves with Cream Gravy, 231
Duck, Roast with Raspberry Sauce, 232
Dumplings and Chicken, 218
-E-
Easy Egg Custard Pie, 319
Easy Pie Crust, 315
EGG(S)
Brunch, 121
Brunch Puff, 134
Cheese Strata, 136
Cheesy Bake, 248
Creole, 122
Easy Custard Pie, 319
Egg Nog, Ginger's, 36
Fancy Scramble, 123
Quiche (See Separate Listing)
Rolls, 24
Shrimp, 122
Soufflé (See Separate Listing)
EGGPLANT
and Curried Chicken Stew, 224
Golden Casserole, 260
Tomato Bake, 278
Vegetable Medley Soup, 59
Enchilada Cheese Towers, 170
-F-
Face Paint, Halloween, 384
Feta Cheese and Shrimp Linguine, 363
Feta Cheese Tart, 137
FETTUCCINI
Chicken Scallopini, 220
Scallops in Herb Sauce, 151
Spinach, 124
with Asparagus, 124
Filet Mignon with Fresh Mushroom Sauce, 174
FISH (Also See Individual Fish Listings)
Crunchy Fried, 141
Curried Fish Soup, 360
Delicious Baked, 160
Stuffed Fish Fillets, 149
FLANK STEAK
Tournedos, 175

with Fresh Basil-Tomato Sauce, 176
with Rice, Oriental, 174
Fondue, Caramel Apple, 354
French Bread, Cheese, 99
French Toast, Fabulous, 117
French Vinaigrette Dressing, 94
Fried Chicken with Cream Gravy, 203
FROSTINGS AND FILLINGS
Amaretto, 333
Chocolate-Cinnamon, 305
Chocolate Glaze, 311
Cream, 295
Cream Cheese, 312
Lane, 306
Lemon, 332
Orange, 325
Pecan Cream Cheese, 307
Sweet Chocolate, 302
Sweet Cream Cheese, 301
Walnut, 310
FRUIT (Also See Individual Fruit Listings and Salads: Fruit)
Almond Curried, 290
Kabobs, Fancy, 352
Plum Chutney, 268
Fudge, Marshmallow Brownies, 330
Fussilli Pescatore, 129

-G-
GAME (See Individual Game Listings)
GARLIC
Cheese Ball, 16
Olives, 24
Roasted Potatoes, 284
Shrimp in Lemon Wine Sauce, 359
Squash, 368
Gazpacho, Chilled, 362
Gazpacho Verde, 43
Ginger Grilled London Broil, 177
Ginger Soufflé, 343
Gingerbread Men, 324
Goulash, Polynesian, 239
Granola, Homemade, 365
GREEN BEANS
Bean Medley, 68
Casserole, 261
Herbed, 277
Hot Marinated, 277
Open Sesame, 276
Green Chiles, Baked, 274
GIFTS
Almond Roca, 379
Amaretto Sauce, 353

Bouquet Garni, 52
Candied Citrus Pecans, 16
Candy Cane Cookies, 342
Caramel Apple Fondue, 354
Caramel Corn Jacks, 382
Cheese Straws, 17
Chocolate Bonbons, 335
Chocolate Truffles, 337
Chocolate Zucchini Bread, 100
Cranberry Orange Tea Bread, 101
Crisp Cucumber Pickles, 68
Decaffinated Spiced Tea Mix, 33
English Toffee, 336
Five Minute Microwave Croutons, 117
Fruited Curry Rice Mix, 130
Garlic Olives, 24
Glazed Nuts, 15
Herbed Butter, 118
Herb Rice Blend, 381
Holiday Cheese Ball, 13
Homemade Croutons, 50
Homemade Granola, 365
Homemade Yogurt, 366
Hot and Sweet Mustard, 230
Hot Buttered Rum Mix, 32
Hot Mocha Mix, 35
Irish Raisin Bread, 104
Mimi's Bar-B-Que Sauce, 191
Mimi's Tomato Relish, 280
Orange-Anise Spice Bags, 38
Peanut Logs, 336
Peachtree Potpourri, 379
Pecan Pralines, 337
Plum Chutney, 268
Poppy Seed Bread, 105
Praline Parfait Sauce, 354
Strawberry Bread, 106
Vegetable Rice, 381
GREEK
Grecian Potato Salad, 73
Manuel's Salad, 72
Shrimp Ala Grecque, 157
Tomato and Pepper Salad, 82
GRILLED
Amberjack, 141
Cornish Hens with Apricot Glaze, 230
Ginger London Broil, 177
Marinated Tuna with Fresh Ginger and Soy Butter, 163
Po Boy Fillets, 172
Rotisserie Turkey for Gas

Grill, 234
Steak Tournedos, 175
Zesty Swordfish, 164
GRITS
Herb Cheese, 132
Willard Scott's Cheese
Soufflé, 132
GROUND BEEF (See Beef,
Ground)

-H-
Hollandaise Sauce, "Hunker
Down" Foolproof, 292
HAM
and Artichoke Casserole,
248
and Cheese Bread, 101
and Pasta Salad, 67
Baked Mornay, 249
Company Casserole, 250
Crescent Squares, 184
Honey-Glazed Baked, 186
Mandarin Rolls, 185
New Orleans Muffaletto,
186
Veggie Slices, 187
Hawaiian Chicken Wings,
17
Haystacks, 295
HEALTH AND DIET
Barley Pilaf, 368
Beef Dijon, 369
Bran Muffins, 362
Brandied Poached Pears,
375
Broiled Zucchini, 367
Ceviche, 358
Chicken and Vegetable
Sauté, 371
Chicken Chow Mein, 370
Chicken Florentine, 226
Chilled Gazpacho, 362
Chocolate Silk, 374
Cold Cucumber Soup with
Dill, 361
Curried Chicken Salad,
370
Curried Fish Soup, 360
Elegant Snapper, 364
Garlic Shrimp in Lemon-
Wine Sauce, 359
Garlic Squash, 368
Glenda's Garden, 369
Homemade Granola, 365
Homemade Yogurt, 366
Low-Cal Macaroni and
Cheese, 373
Mandarin Orange and
Almond Salad, 357
Orange and Lemon Salad,
359
Sesame-Citrus Green
Salad, 371
Shrimp and Feta Cheese
Linguine, 363

Snappy Vegetable Dip,
358
Spinach Pasta with
Mushroom Cheese
Sauce, 372
Strawberry Pie, 376
Strawberry Surprise, 366
Stuffed Potatoes, 367
Tarragon Chicken Salad,
364
Tomato and Cheese Salad,
363
Tomato-Zucchini Salad,
373
Tuna Spread, 360
Veal Scallopini with
Marsala Wine, 372
White Wine Custard, 376
Yellow Squash Pecan Pie,
375
Yogurt Pops, 361
Hearts of Palm Salad, 81
Herb Butter, 118
Herb Cheese Bread, 98
Herb Cheese Grits, 132
Herb Rice Blend, 381
Herb Tomato Bread, 103
Herbed Green Beans, 277
HONEY
Almond Dressing, 92
Dressing, 92
Glazed Baked Ham, 186
Mustard Dressing, 93
Puffs, 327
Wheat Rolls, 113

-I-
ICE CREAM
Chocolate Roll, 346
Clay's Favorite Pie, 319
Hot Buttered Rum Mix, 32
Kahlua Velvet Frosty, 36
Nutty Buddy, 348
Pistachio Ice Cream Pie,
321
Quick Mud Pie, 320
INTERNATIONAL (Also See
Greek, Irish, Italian,
Mexican and Oriental)
Brown Bread, 99
Chicken Waterzooi, 49
Munich "Sauerbraten",
179
Peloponnesian Pasta
Salad, 76
IRISH
Irish Raisin Bread, 104
Irish Style Corned Beef
and Cabbage, 183
ITALIAN
Italian Cheese Rolls, 14
Chicken Scalloppini, 220
Holiday Antipasto, 12
Risotto-"Italian Rice", 130
-J-
Jambalaya, Hoppinjohn, 196

-K-
Kabobs, Beef-Chicken, 171
Kabobs, Fancy Fruit, 352
Kahlua Supreme, 350
Key Lime Pie, 320
KIDS
Bird Feeder Candles, 384
Candy Cane Cookies, 342
Caramel Corn Jacks, 382
Cheese Bread Sticks, 100
Chicken Nuggets, 204
Chocolate Bonbons, 335
Christmas Tree Cones, 312
Colored Popcorn Balls,
352
Dandy-Quicky
Doughnuts, 102
Flower Potcakes, 300
Frozen Strawberry Yogurt
Salad, 91
Gingerbread Men, 324
Halloween Face Paint, 384
Haystacks, 295
Ice Cream Muffins, 98
Instant Non-Toxic Paste,
384
Lasagnette, 169
Lollipops, 308
Modeling Clay, 383
New Orleans Muffaletto,
186
No-Bake Play Dough, 383
Nutty Buddy, 348
Patriotic Pastries, 380
Peanut Play Dough, 380
Popcorn Balls, 382
Red Candy Apples, 339
Saltine Treats, 380
Silly Putty, 383
Soft Pretzels, 118
Spanish Squares, 285
Strawberry Surprise, 366
Stuffed Apples, 88
Super Salad, 86
Yogurt Pops, 361
Kiwi Orange Salad, 90
Korean Salad, Dressing for,
94

-L-
LAMB
Butterflied Leg of, 189
Princess Diana Roast
Saddle of, 188
Sweet and Sour, 251
Sweet Chops, 190
Lasagna, Chicken for a
Crowd, 243
Lasagnette, 169
LEMON
and Orange Salad, 359
Chicken, 205
Frozen Delight, 350
Ice Box Pie, 322

Lime Soufflé, 87
Tangy Mold, 85
Lima Bean Medley, 68
Lima Beans, Barbecued, 278
Lime-Lemon Soufflé, 87
LINGUINI
Feta Cheese and Shrimp, 363
Salad, 74
Trotters' with Crabmeat, 143
Liver, Delicious Pate, 25
LOBSTER
Asparagus Cocktail Mousse, 10
Pasta Seafood Salad, 69
Thermidor, 150
Lo-Cal Macaroni and Cheese, 373
Lollipops, 308
London Broil, Ginger Grilled, 177
London Broil, Marinade for, 177

-M-
MACARONI
and Cheese, Deluxe, 136
and Cheese, Low-Cal, 373
and Cheese Salad, 78
Do-Ahead Seafood Bake, 254
Million Dollar Salad, 78
with Wine and Cheese, 135
Maple-Pecan Chicken, 208
MARINADE
for Beef-Chicken Kabobs, 171
for Butterflied Leg of Lamb, 189
for London Broil, 177
for Roast Tenderloin, 182
for Sweet Lamb Chops, 190
Marinated Asparagus, 267
Marinated Green Beans, Hot, 277
Marinated Roast Beef Sandwiches, 178
Marinated Vegetables, 31
Meatballs and Bar-B-Que Spareribs, 192
Meatballs, Cranberry, 9
MEXICAN
Baked Green Chilies, 274
Chalupas, 196
Chili Relleno Dip, 23
Chili Relleno Casserole, 247
Chilled Gazpacho, 362
Enchilada Cheese Towers, 170
Enchilada Soup, 50

Hot Nacho Dip, 22
Queso, 138
Salad, 66
Sopa De Pollo Y Maíz, 46
MICROWAVE
Artichoke Soup, 51
Cheesy Potato Soup, 54
Chicken with Sherried Cheese Sauce, 212
MOUSSE
Amaretto, 338
Asparagus-Lobster Cocktail, 10
Curry Chicken, 207
Salmon, 27
Shrimp, 29
MUFFINS
Bran, 362
Ice Cream, 98
Peach, 108
Pineapple Bran, 109
Six Week Bran, 110
Sweet Potatoes, 108
Munich "Sauerbraten", 179
MUSHROOM(S)
and Almonds with Wild Rice, 131
and Leek Salad, 75
Chiffy Chaffy, 287
in Mustard Cream, 279
Marinated Mushroom Salad, 75
Phyllo Pastries, 18
Squares, 25
Mustard, Hot and Sweet, 230

-N-
New Orleans Muffaletto, 186
NOODLE(S)
Baked Ham Mornay, 249
Ground Beef Bake, 239
Poulet Au Frommage, 246
Pudding with Fruit, 339
Soy Baked Chicken, 227
Veal Stroganoff, 257
Nuts (Also See Individual Nut Listings)
Cocoa Layer Cake, 302
Orange Date Bars, 331
Pineapple Banana Cake, 301

-O-
OKRA
Chicken Gumbo, 48
Pilaf, 281
Tomato Bake, 280
Olive and Cream Cheese Ball, 14
Olives, Garlic, 24
ONION(S)
and Peas, Creamed, 281
and Proscuitto Bread, 106
Broccoli-Stuffed Vidalia, 270

Casserole, 261
Parmesan Canapès, 21
Rye, 21
ORANGE
Almond Chicken, 217
and Lemon Salad, 359
Anise Spice Bags, 38
Cranberry Tea Bread, 101
Date-Nut Bars, 331
Frosted Salad, 85
Kiwi Salad, 90
Mandarin and Almond Salad, 357
Marinated Salad, 90
Pecan Shortbread Cookies, 325
with Brown Rice-Pecan Salad, 80
ORIENTAL
Barbara Dooley's Stir-Fry Shrimp with Fried Rice, 159
Cashew Chicken, 244
Chicken and Peanuts in Hot Sauce, 224
Chicken Salad, 63
Chicken Chow Mein, 370
Chicken Sukh, 228
Egg Rolls, 24
Far East Shrimp Balls, 30
Flank Steak with Rice, 174
Mandarin Ham Rolls, 185
Sesame Chicken Dinner, 226
Soy Baked Chicken, 227
Spaghetti, 238
Stuffed Chicken Teriyaki, 229
Sukiyaki, 173
Orzo Stuffed Roast Chicken, 213
OYSTERS
Artichoke Soup, 51
Log, 28
New Orleans Sandwich, 147
Rockefeller Casserole, 146
Scalloped, 148

-P-
Parmesan Chicken, Sherried, 211
Parmesan Shrimp Scampi, 158
PASTA (Also See Individual Pasta Listings)
and Ham Salad, 67
Crawfish Monica, 146
Minestrone Alphabet Soup with Pesto, 53
Pesto and, 126
Seafood Salad, 69
Shrimp and Fresh Basil, 127
Tarragon Chicken with

Angel Hair, 214
Vegetable Medley, 128
with Clam Sauce, 126
Paste, Instant Non-Toxic, 384
PEAS
and Onions, Creamed, 281
Bean Medley, 68
Green Medley, 287
Scoville, 283
Split Soup with Smoked Ham, 52
Tangy English Mold, 81
PEACH(ES)
Glazed Almond Cake, 303
Molded Cream and, 88
Muffins, 108
Wonderful Cobbler, 324
Peachtree Potpourri, 379
PEANUT BUTTER
Nutty Buddy, 348
Peanut Logs, 336
Play Dough, 380
Saltine Treats, 380
Stuffed Apples, 88
Pears, Baked with Caramel, 351
Pears, Brandied Poached, 375
PECAN(S)
Angel Pie, 322
Apple Upside-Down Pie, 316
Breaded Chicken, 216
Candied Citrus, 16
Glazed Nuts, 15
Maple Chicken, 208
Mystery Pie, 323
No-Fail Pie, 321
Orange Shortbread Cookies, 325
Pralines, 337
Seafood, 158
Yellow Squash Pie, 375
Pepper and Tomato Salad, Greek, 82
Pepper and Tomato Soup, Roasted, 58
Pesto and Pasta, 126
Picadillo, 181
Pickles, Crisp Cucumber, 68
PICNIC
Beef Salad with Broccoli and Asparagus, 64
Bessie's Chicken, 202
Ceviche, 358
Cheese Bread Sticks, 100
Chicken and Artichoke Rice Salad, 63
Chicken Nuggets, 204
Chiffy Chaffy, 287
Chilled Gazpacho, 362
Cold Cucumber Soup, 54
Gazpacho Verde, 43
Green Pea Medley, 287

Honey Glazed Baked Ham, 186
Marinated Asparagus, 267
Marinated Roast Beef Sandwiches, 178
Mushrooms in Mustard Cream, 279
Salami, 172
Sesame Chicken with Honey Dip, 220
Shrimp and Feta Cheese Linguine, 363
Tree Top Marinade, 82
Tuna Spread, 360
PIE
Amaretto, 314
Angel Pecan, 322
Apple Upside-Down, 316
Baker's Chocolate, 314
Black Bottom, 315
Chocolate Rum, 317
Classic Chess, 317
Clay's Favorite Ice Cream, 319
Coconut Cream, 318
Easy Egg Custard, 319
Key Lime, 320
Lemon Ice Box, 322
Mystery Pecan, 323
No-Fail Pecan, 321
Pineapple Chess, 318
Pistachio Ice Cream, 321
Savory Baked Corn, 274
Sour Cream-Pumpkin, 323
Strawberry, 376
Sweet Potato, 326
Wonderful Peach Cobbler, 324
Yellow Squash Pecan, 375
Pie Crust, Easy, 315
Pilaf, Barley, 368
Pilaf, Okra, 281
PINEAPPLE
Banana-Nut Cake, 301
Bran Muffins, 109
Champagne Punch, 34
Chess Pie, 318
Cream Delight, 351
Party Casserole, 291
Super Salad, 86
Pistachio Ice Cream Pie, 321
Play Dough, No-Cook, 383
Plum Chutney, 268
Po Boy Fillets, 172
Polynesian Goulash, 239
Popcorn Balls, 382
Popcorn Balls, Colored, 352
Poppy Seed Bread, 105
Poppy Seed Chicken, 211
PORK
Bar-B-Que Spareribs and Meatballs, 192
Beef Stuffed Roast, 193
Bob's Brunswick Stew, 167

Braised Tenderloin, 190
Brunswick Stew,, 168
Cashew Chicken, 244
Chalupas, 196
Chops with Sour Cream, 194
Favorite Chops in Casserole, 250
Mimi's Bar-B-Que, 191
Oriental Spaghetti, 238
Porky's Revenge, 194
Roasted Pork Loin with Prunes and Madeira, 195
Sausage (See Separate Listing)
Stuffed Chicken Teriyaki, 229
POTATO(ES)
Cheesy Casserole, 283
Cheesy Microwave, 54
Confetti Salad, 79
Garlic Roasted, 284
Grecian Salad, 73
Overnight, 284
Parisienne, 282
Peachtree Balls, 282
Salad with Sour Cream Dressing, 79
Scalloped Au Gratin, 262
Stuffed, 367
POULTRY (See Individual Poultry Listings)
Praline Parfait Sauce, 354
Pralines, Pecan, 337
Pretzels, Soft, 118
Prosciutto and Onion Bread, 106
Prunes and Apricot Coffeecake, 116
PUDDING
Chocolate Silk, 374
Grandma's Corn, 275
Noodle with Fruit, 339
Rum Pudding Kristine, 340
Yia Yia's Rice, 338
PUMPKIN
Baked Stuffed, 291
Sour Cream Pie, 323
Squares, 334
PUNCH (See Beverages: Punch)

-Q-
Queso, 138
Quiche, Easy Swiss Cheese, 138
Quiche, Irresistible Spinach, 135
Quick Mud Pie, 320
-R-
Raisin Bread, Irish, 104
Raisin Stuffed Apples, 88
Relish, Mimi's Tomato, 280

RESTAURANT
Baked Stuffed Snapper, 162
Bessie's Chicken, 202
Bob's Brunswick Stew, 167
Bone's Beer-Battered Shrimp, 153
Bone's Seafood Seasoning, 164
Breast of Chicken Florentine, 222
Chestnut Cheesecake, 300
Chocolate Chocolate Crepes, 345
Chocolate Marquis, 348
Chocolate Snowball, 349
Chocolate Truffle Cake, 304
Corn Sticks, 110
Crawfish Soufflé, 145
Creole Eggs, 122
Feta Cheese Tart, 137
Frozen Chocolate Parfait, 347
Fussilli Pescatore, 129
Ginger Soufflé, 343
Glenda's Garden 369
Grilled Amberjack, 141
Lobster Thermidor, 150
Manuel's Greek Salad, 72
Orange Marinated Fruit Salad, 90
Pasta Seafood Salad, 69
Pearl's Fried Crabmeat Puffs, 144
Potato Salad with Sour Cream Dressing, 79
Salmon Mousse, 27
Shrimp and Fresh Basil Pasta, 127
Stuffed Chicken Breasts with Dill Butter Sauce, 206
Sweet Rolls From Herren's, 115
Swiss Cheese Soufflé, 133
Tamara Salata, 31
The Georgian Club Caesar Salad and Dressing, 70
The Market's Crusty Bread, 102
Trotters' Linguini with Crabmeat, 143
Trotters' Seafood Soup, 56
RICE
Baked, 262
Barbara Dooley's Stir-Fry Shrimp with Fried, 159
Blend of the Bayou Seafood Casserole, 253
Brazillan, 129
Brown Rice-Pecan Salad with Oranges, 80
Cashew Chicken, 244

Chicken and Artichoke Salad, 63
Chicken and Peanuts in Hot Sauce, 224
Chicken Breasts in Currant Jelly Sauce, 216
Chicken-Casserole Delight, 244
Chicken Elegante, 246
Chicken Sukh, 228
Company Ham Casserole, 250
French Garden Soup, 55
Fruited Curry Mix, 130
Herb Blend, 381
Main Dish Salad, 66
One Meal Dish, 241
Orange Almond Chicken, 217
Oriental Sesame Chicken Dinner, 226
Risotto-"Italian Rice", 130
Sausage Casserole, 252
Seafood Casserole, 255
Shrimp and Crab Rice Casserole, 256
Shrimp Creole, 154
Shrimp Perlo, 156
Smoked Sausage Salad Medley, 71
Stuffed Chicken Teriyaki, 229
Tangy Baked Chicken, 214
Vegetable, 381
Wild Chicken Salad, 64
Wild Stuffing with Roast Turkey, 233
Wild with Mushrooms and Almonds, 131
with Green Chiles, 128
with Thyme, 131
Yia Yia's, 338
Ripe Olive and Artichoke Salad, 76
Roast Beef for Sandwiches, 178
Roast Chicken Stuffed with Orzo, 213
Roast Duck with Raspberry Sauce, 232
Roast Tenderloin, 182
Roast Turkey with Wild Rice Stuffing, 233
Roasted Pork Loin with Prunes and Madeira, 195
ROLLS
Butter, 114
Fan Up, 112
Honey Wheat, 113
Sweet From Herren's, 115
Rotelle with Ground Beef, Baked, 125
Rum Pudding Kristine, 340
-S-

SALAD(S)
Fruit
Green and Gold, 72
Kiwi Orange, 90
Mandarin Orange and Almond, 357
Orange and Lemon Salad, 359
Orange Marinated, 90
Sesame-Citrus Green Salad, 371
Super, 86
Fruit; Congealed
Congealed Cranberry Surprise, 84
Frosted Orange, 85
Holiday Cranberry Mold, 84
Lemon-Lime Soufflé, 87
Molded Peaches and Cream, 88
Molded Waldorf, 89
Pretzel, 86
Strawberry Rosé, 89
Tangy Lemon Mold, 85
Fruit; Frozen
Cranberry Dream, 83
Strawberry Yogurt, 91
Meat/Seafood
Beef Salad with Broccoli and Asparagus, 64
Chicken and Artichoke Rice, 63
Crab Avocado, 142
Curried Chicken, 370
Curried Seafood, 160
Ham and Pasta, 67
Hot Chicken Casserole, 242
Insalata Romana, 65
Main Dish Rice Salad, 66
Mexican, 66
Oriental Chicken, 63
Pasta Seafood, 69
Smoked Sausage Medley, 71
Tarragon Chicken, 364
Wild Rice Chicken, 64
Pasta/Rice
Brown Rice-Pecan with Oranges, 80
Chicken and Artichoke Rice, 63
Ham and Pasta, 67
Linguini, 74
Macaroni and Cheese, 78
Main Dish Rice, 66
Million Dollar Macaroni, 78
Peloponnesian Pasta, 76
Wild Rice Chicken, 64
Vegetable/ Tossed Green
Bean Medley, 68
Broccoli Mold, 74

Confetti Potato, 79
Corn, 71
Fresh Vegetable,
    Marinade, 83
Grecian Potato, 73
Greek Tomato and
    Pepper, 82
Hearts of Palm Salad, 81
Kiwi Orange, 90
Manuel's Greek, 72
Marinated Mushroom,
    75
Mimosa, 77
Mushroom and Leek, 75
Potato with Sour Cream
    Dressing, 79
Ripe Olive and
    Artichoke, 76
Strawberry Spinach, 91
The Georgian Club
    Caesar and Dressing,
    70
Tomato and Cheese, 363
Tomato-Zuccini, 373
Tree Top Marinade, 82
Vegetable: Congealed
    Broccoli Mold, 74
Tangy English Pea Mold,
    81
SALAD DRESSING
    Almond-Honey, 92
    Buttermilk-Garlic, 93
    Curry, 73
    Dill, 67
    French Vinaigrette, 94
    Ginger, 65
    Honey, 92
    Honey-Mustard, 93
    Manuel's Greek, 72
    Mimosa, 77
    Oil and Vinegar, 76
    Poppy Seed, 91
    Rebecca Sauce, 27
    Sesame Oil and Vinegar,
    357
    Sweet and Sour, 94
    The Georgian Club
    Caesar, 70
Salami, 172
Salmon In Foil, 148
Salmon Mousse, 27
Salmon Rolls, 28
SANDWICHES
    Cream Cheese and Bacon
    Tea, 10
    Glenda's Garden, 369
    Marinated Roast Beef, 178
    New Orleans Muffaletto,
    186
    New Orleans Oyster, 147
    Roast Beef for, 178
SAUCES
    Amaretto, 353

Cheddar Cheese, 123
Chocolate, 346
Cream, 121
Currant Jelly Sauce, 216
Dill Butter Sauce, 206
Dill, 27
for Commander Burn's
    Barbecue Chicken, 208
Fresh Basil-Tomato, 176
Fresh Mushroom, 174
Ginger and Soy-Butter,
    163
Grand Marnier, 353
"Hunker Down" Foolproof
    Hollandaise Sauce, 292
Honey-Mustard Sauce,
    144
Horseradish, 183
Lemon-Mustard, 188
Lemon-Wine Sauce for
    Garlic Shrimp, 359
Mimi's Barbeque, 191
Mornay, 268
Mushroom-Wine for
    Chicken, 210
Neta's Chive, 292
Parmesan Cheese, 123
Praline Parfait, 354
Raspberry, 340
Rebecca, 27
Sherried-Cheese, 212
Sweet and Tangy Dipping
    153
Tangy Barbeque, 193
White, 125, 222
Sauerbraten, Munich, 179
SAUSAGE
    Frogmore Stew, 155
    Hoppinjohn Jambalaya,
    196
    Hearty Bean Soup, 43
    Party Pizzas, 26
    Pinwheels, 22
    Rice Casserole, 252
    Smoked Salad Medley, 71
Sautéed Fresh Vegetables,
    270
Sautéed Spinach, 286
Scallopini, Chicken, 220
Scalloped Artichokes, 267
Scalloped Carrots, 273
Scalloped Oysters, 148
Scalloped Potatoes Au
    Gratin, 262
SCALLOPS
    Ceviche, 358
    in Herb Sauce, 151
    Fussilli Pescatore, 129
    Seafood Pecan, 158
    Seafood Stew, 154
    Seafood Supreme, 152
    Trotters' Seafood Soup, 56
Scotched Filet Mignon with

Fresh Mushroom Sauce,
    174
SEAFOOD (Also See
    Individual Seafood List-
    ings)
    Blend of the Bayou
    Casserole, 253
    Casserole, 255
    Ceviche, 358
    Curried Salad, 160
    Do-Ahead Bake, 254
    Fussilli Pescatore, 129
    Pasta Salad, 69
    Pecan, 158
    Seasoning, Bone's, 164
    Soup, 56
    Stew, 154
    Supreme, 152
    Trotters' Soup, 56
SEASONINGS
    Bone's Seafood, 164
    Bouquet Garni, 52
    Chili, 198
Sesame-Citrus Green Salad,
    371
Sherried Parmesan Chicken,
    211
Sherried Sweet Potatoes, 288
Sherry Sour, 39
SHRIMP
    a la Grecque, 157
    and Crab Rice Casserole,
    256
    and Feta Cheese Linguine,
    363
    and Fresh Basil Pasta, 127
    Barbara Dooley's Stir-Fry
    with Fried Rice, 159
    Bone's Beer-Battered, 153
    Company Seafood Dinner,
    254
    Crawfish Soufflé, 145
    Creole, 154
    Eggs, 122
    Far East Balls, 30
    Frogmore Stew, 155
    Garlic in Lemon-Wine
    Sauce, 359
    Hidden Treasure, 26
    Main Dish Rice Salad, 66
    Manallé, 156
    Mousse, 29
    Parmesan Scampi, 158
    Pasta Seafood Salad, 69
    Perlo, 156
    Pickled, 29
    Pizza, 30
    Trotters' Seafood Soup, 56
SIDE DISHES
    Almond Curried Fruit, 290
    Baked Stuffed Pumpkin,
    291
    Hot Apricot Casserole, 290

My Mother's Apples and
Cornflakes, 289
Party Pineapple Casserole,
291
Silly Putty, 383
SIRLOIN
Beer Beef Steak
Stroganoff, 180
Steak in a Bag, 180
Sukiyaki, 173
SNAPPER
Almondine, 161
Baked Stuffed, 162
Elegant, 364
Sneaky Petes, 37
SOUFFLÉ
Blue Cheese, 133
Crawfish, 145
Ginger, 343
Lemon-Lime, 87
Sweet Potato, 288
Swiss Cheese, 133
Willard Scott's Cheese
Grits, 132
SOUPS
Artichoke, 51
Bouquet Garni, 52
Broccoli-Cheese Supreme,
44
Cheesy Chicken Noodle,
47
Cheesy Microwave Potato,
54
Chicken Gumbo, 48
Chicken Waterzooi, 49
Chilled Gazpacho, 362
Chilled Creamy Avocado,
60
Chowder (See Separate
Listing)
Cold Cucumber with Dill,
361
Creamy Cucumber-
Spinach, 55
Curried Fish, 360
Cold Cucumber, 54
Enchilada, 50
French Garden, 55
Gazpacho Verde, 43
Hearty Sausage-Bean, 43
Minestrone Alphabet with
Pesto, 53
Roasted Pepper and
Tomato, 58
Seafood, 56
Sopa De Pollo Y Maiz, 46
Split Pea with Smoked
Ham, 52
Sweet and Sour, 44
Trotters' Seafood, 56
Turnip Green and Cream,
58
Vegetable Medley, 59
Sour Cream-Pumpkin Pie,
323

Southern Chicken Pie, 223
Soy Baked Chicken, 227
Spaghetti, Oriental, 238
SPINACH
Bread, 104
Breast of Chicken
Florentine, 222
Cheesy Casserole, 285
Chicken Florentine, 226
Crab Grass, 20
Creamy Cucumber Soup,
55
Fettuccini, 124
Irresistible Quiche, 135
Oysters Rockefeller
Casserole, 146
Pasta with Mushroom-
Cheese Sauce, 372
Sautéed, 286
Strawberry Salad, 91
Squares, 285
SQUASH
Casserole, 263
Cheesy Dressing, 286
Chiffy Chaffy, 287
Garlic, 368
Yellow Pecan Pie, 375
Zucchini (See Separate
Listing)
STEW
Bob's Brunswick, 167
Brunswick, 168
Chicken Waterzooi, 49
Curried Chicken and
Eggplant, 224
Frogmore, 155
Seafood, 154
STRAWBERRY(IES)
Angel Cake, 309
Bavarian Cream, 344
Bread, 106
Cardinal, 352
Cheese Ball, 16
Colonial Cake, 308
Fresh in Grand Marnier
Sauce, 353
Frozen Yogurt Salad, 91
Pie, 376
Pretzel Salad, 86
Spinach Salad, 91
Rosé, 89
Super Salad, 86
Stroganoff, Beer Beef Steak,
180
Stroganoff, Veal, 257
Stuffed Chicken Breasts with
Dill Butter Sauce, 206
Stuffed Potatoes, 367
Sukiyaki, 173
Sweet and Sour Dressing, 94
Sweet and Sour Lamb, 251
SWEET POTATO(ES)
Muffins, 108
Pie, 326
Sherried, 288

Soufflé, 288
SWISS CHEESE
Baked Chicken, 201
Chicken, 219
Easy Pie, 138
Soufflé, 133
Swordfish, Zesty Grilled, 164
-T-
Tarragon Chicken Salad, 364
Tarragon Chicken with Angel
Hair Pasta, 214
TEA (See Beverages: Tea)
Tenderloin, Roast, 182
Tequila-Champagne Punch,
38
Teriyaki, Stuffed Chicken,
229
Toffee, English, 336
TOMATO(ES)
and Cheese Salad, 363
and Pepper Salad, Greek,
82
and Roasted Pepper Soup,
58
Broccoli-Stuffed, 269
Cheese Casserole, 263
Eggplant Bake, 278
Herb Bread, 103
Mimi's Relish, 280
Okra Bake, 280
Zucchini Salad, 373
TORTES
Torte, Almond, 313
Torte, Coffee Brownie, 311
TUNA
and Artichokes, 256
Grilled Marinated with
Fresh Ginger and Soy-
Butter Sauce, 163
Insalata Romana, 65
Spread, 360
TURKEY
Crescent Squares, 184
Roast with Wild Rice
Stuffing, 233
Rotisserie Grilled for a Gas
Grill, 234
Southern, Pie, 223
Turnip Greens and Cream
Soup, 58
Turnip Greens, Grandma's,
289

-V-
VEAL
Sauté De Veau Marengo,
258
Scallopini with Marsala
Wine, 372
Stroganoff Casserole, 257
Vermouth, 198
with Mustard Sauce, 197
VEGETABLE(S) (Also See
Individual Vegetable List-
ings)

and Chicken Sauté, 371
Glenda's Garden, 369
Marinated, 31
Medley Soup, 59
Minestrone Alphabet Soup
  with Pesto, 53
Pasta Medley, 128
Ratatouille, 264
Rice, 381
Sautéed Fresh, 270
Snappy Dip, 358
Stuffed Ham Slices, 187
Vinaigrette Dressing, French,
  94
-W-
WALNUT(S)
  Glazed Bacon with, 11

Glazed Nuts, 15
Yule Log, 310
Whiskey-Glazed Corned
  Beef, 184
Wine, Hot Spiced, 40
Wine, White Custard, 376
Wine, White Sangria, 36
WOK
  Barbara Dooley's Stir-Fry
    Shrimp with Fried Rice,
    159
  Chicken and Peanuts in
    Hot Sauce, 224
  Chicken Chow Mein, 370
  Far East Shrimp Balls, 30
  Mandarin Ham Rolls, 185
  Oriental Sesame Chicken

Dinner, 226
Sukiyaki, 173
-Y-
YOGURT
  Frozen Cranberry Dream
    Salad, 83
  Frozen Strawberry Salad,
    91
  Homemade, 366
  Pops, 361
-Z-
ZUCCHINI
  and Corn, 275
  Broiled, 367
  Chocolate Bread, 100
  Ground Beef Bake, 242
  Tomato Salad, 373